URBAN RENEWAL AND AMERICAN CITIES
The Dilemma of Democratic Intervention

An advanced study in political science

URBAN RENEWAL AND AMERICAN CITIES

The Dilemma of Democratic Intervention

SCOTT GREER

The Center for Metropolitan Studies, Northwestern University

THE BOBBS-MERRILL COMPANY, INC.
A Subsidiary of Howard W. Sams & Co., Inc.
PUBLISHERS   *Indianapolis • New York • Kansas City*

Robert C. Wood
CONSULTING EDITOR
The Massachusetts Institute of Technology

Contents

Preface

In this essay I have attempted to survey a complex program already spread among hundreds of American cities. Each city is in some respects unique, as is each local public authority and program. Working alone, I could only sample a few cities and talk with a few responsible officials out of the hundreds involved. I am certain that my ignorance far outweighs my knowledge.

Nevertheless, I have put my findings and my conclusions in unambiguous terms, for several reasons. First, I think certain aspects of the program do not require an elaborate sampling scheme: They are integral parts of the beast, wherever he comes to earth. There is, after all, only one federal government, one urban renewal administration, and one current Housing Act. Secondly, I think there is virtue in a straightforward, even if dogmatic, presentation of conclusions. The argument stands forth with greater clarity. Thirdly, and kin to this latter point, I feel that urban renewal will gain more at present from central questions of central purpose than from a highly qualified memorandum of impressions.

One reason for my inability to prove some of my conclusions is our general ignorance of the program's outline and effects. This is partly due to the youth and retarded development of the program, partly to the administrative blindness built in by a Congress that will spend billions of dollars for action and not a cent for research. (See Chapter 8.) Another reason for my inability to prove strong statements is, simply, that some statements rest upon one's commitments to values, not upon one's estimate of facts. My own commitments are, generally, to an increase in the range of social choice, for individuals and for communities. In the process, I would like to see a more general acknowledgment of the inevitability of governmental action in a large-scale society, and more general concern for *social innovation,* which might improve that action in its competence and in its responsibility to broader values.

The urban renewal officials, who helped me to understand the program through discussing with me their problems and their goals, are equally committed to broader values. They are Americans and public servants, and proud to be. The quality of these persons and the integrity of their dedication to the public business I found impressive and moving. So, I believe, would the reader. Yet I sometimes found their programs questionable and their achievements ambiguous in the light of my own judgment. I also found an undercurrent of genuine intellectual concern and uneasiness among them. Because I am on their side in believing we must be inventive, committed, responsible for our collective destiny, I feel this essay is not an attack upon them individually or as a professional group. I have tried to concern myself with urban renewal as a very large, very radical program venturing into unknown territory, one whose basic ambiguities are reflected in their own day-to-day problems. Indeed, the local public authority (LPA) officials are vividly aware of these connections. I remember one perplexed man, who finally thought aloud: "Do you suppose it's the people, or the way the damned system works?" Because I think it is largely "the way the damned system works" I have ventured, as a political sociologist, to try to describe and analyze that system.

My field observation and interviewing took place during 1961–1962, in the following cities: Boston; Chicago; Eugene, Oregon; Los

Angeles; Little Rock, Arkansas; Milwaukee; Miami; New Orleans; North Little Rock, Arkansas; Pittsburgh; Saint Louis; San Francisco; Tacoma, Washington; and Springfield, Oregon. I also spent brief but intensive periods of fieldwork in San Juan, Puerto Rico, and Kingston, Jamaica. The latter cities not only gave me some perspective on "un-American" housing problems, but also threw into sharp relief the very high standards for housing that are official policy in the fifty states. They also reinforced belief in the great importance of governmental structure in the failure or success of public intervention in the housing market.

Beyond these field experiences I relied upon the published reports of the local public authorities and the Urban Renewal Agency. I also leaned heavily upon certain case studies of urban renewal, particularly the Rossi and Dentler volume, *The Politics of Urban Renewal;* the study of the Boston West End project by Herbert Gans, published as *The Urban Villagers;* and the study of Newark by Harold Kaufman, *Urban Renewal Politics: Slum Clearance in Newark.* I had the privilege of seeing, in manuscript, two recent economic analyses of the urban renewal program, *Housing Markets and Public Policy,* by William Grigsby; and *Economic Evaluation of Urban Renewal: Conceptual Foundation of Benefit-Cost Analysis,* by Jerome Rothenberg. The selected bibliography gives (though inadequately) credit to the wide variety of scholars and spokesmen who helped me develop my own direction through the complex moral and intellectual problem.

In approaching this problem I used the conventional analytic tools of the sociologist. These are concepts that emphasize the coercive effects of the *culture,* the inherited moral (or normative) system. They also emphasize the nature of *social organization* as a set of constraints upon our behavior and a powerful tool of control. Finally, they underline the ubiquity and the scope of *social change,* the vast and cumulative trends in the society.

Culture is the beginning. Here we see the very framework within which the quality of housing and the nature of our cities are defined as "problems." These problems are translated, through the political process, into legally defined programs empowered by laws. But laws are only legitimatized aspirations until they affect the actions of men; to have such effect they must be translated into the efforts of organized social groups. As this occurs, they are subject to all the qualifications that such organization entails—the struggles between line and staff, between local autonomy and centralized administration, between survival tactics and long-run policy. As we shall see, these and many more side-effects occur in the implementation of that legitimatized aspiration called the urban renewal program. The end product, the projects and programs in hundreds of American cities, must then be seen within the framework of massive social trends including, for example, changes in housing standards and supply, in transportation and the layout of cities, in the distribution of income and the segregation of ethnic minorities. Although such trends are hardly produced by the program, they still contain it and set the resistances and opportunities for its achievements.

Thus the structure of this report will be tripartite. The first part is a brief analysis of urban renewal as part of the culture, a result of the interaction between social structure and accepted thinking (Chapters 1 and 2). The second part is an organizational analysis of the program, with an emphasis upon the local public authority as the major locus of action (Chapters 3, 4 and 5). The last consideration is the massive and intertwined social trends that constitute, at a given moment, "the nature of things" (Chapter 6). After this analysis I offer, in the last chapters, such modest proposals as I can for strengthening the program and achieving its goals.

In conclusion, I wish to acknowledge the support of various organizations and individuals. I am most grateful to the dozens of urban renewal officials who assisted me so generously; to such scholars as Robert Agger of the University of Oregon, George Duggar of the University of Pittsburgh, Edward Banfield and James Wilson of Harvard, Henry Schmandt of the University of Wisconsin-Milwaukee, and my colleagues here at Northwestern; to the other members of the Ford Foundation research group on urban renewal. I am also grateful to the Public Affairs Program of the Ford Foundation for their generous financial support. Grateful acknowledgment is made to the American Society of Planning Officials and to the Executive Director, Mr. Dennis O'Harrow, for permission to use portions of my article "Key Issues for the Central City" which was included in their book *Planning 1963* (Interstate, November 1963).

SCOTT GREER

Evanston, Illinois
April 1965

URBAN RENEWAL AND AMERICAN CITIES:
The Dilemma of Democratic Intervention

Chapter 1

AN OVERVIEW OF THE PROGRAM

At a cost of more than three billion dollars the Urban Renewal Agency (URA) has succeeded in materially reducing the supply of low-cost housing in American cities. Like highways and streets, the program has ripped through the neighborhoods of the poor, powered by the right of eminent domain. Slums are being cleared, and bright patches of new construction dot the central areas of the big cities. From Boston to San Francisco, from Portland, Oregon, to Portland, Maine, hundreds of American cities and their citizens are involved. The program is so widespread, so varied, and so complex that few people have more than a skewed random image of it.

We see skid row being renewed out of the path of the bank in one town, the Orthodox synagogue being displaced by the telephone company's new building in another. We see a well-kept and charming neighborhood of working men and their families, where once stood a depressing collection of shacks inhabited by many of the same people. We also see the Italian parishioners, returned to their destroyed neighborhood for the "blessing of the house." Each *pater familias* stands in front of the vacant lot where his house once stood to receive the benediction of the priest. In the Greek neighborhood of Chicago the film, *Goodbye Socrates,* vividly demonstrates some of the costs of the program.

Because it *is* a big program, complex and varied, this study attempts to organize an over-all, birdseye view of it. It does not generalize from one case in one city. Nor does it ignore the complex structure of politics and government, reaching from the halls of Congress to the chambers of the city councils, which initiate and undergird programs in hundreds of cities. Today the program is expanding rapidly, and as it expands there are changes in emphasis and goals. We must be aware of this, for it is a *new* program, still capable of reformulation in terms of its effectiveness as democratic intervention in the shape of cities. Under the Kennedy and Johnson regimes the program has been accelerated; with new and highly committed personnel there is every prospect it will become a part of life in every American city of any size. Since it has already been in operation for fifteen years, it seems fair and useful to take a look at its operations and results.

Because urban renewal is a novel effort, we must look at it from several angles—as an aspiration, as an organization, and as given result. Since it began in the acts of the 81st Congress, and since its possibilities and limits are still derived, finally, from the action of the Congress, we shall begin at the beginning: What are the bare bones, the statutory nature of the urban renewal program?

Objectives and Means

The declaration of national housing policy in the Housing Act of 1949 states the goals of all the various housing agencies, including those of the Urban Renewal Agency.

The Congress hereby declares that the general welfare and security of the Nation and the health and living standards of its people require housing production and related community development sufficient to remedy the serious housing shortage, the elimination of sub-standard and other inadequate housing through the clearance of slums and blighted areas, and the realization as soon as feasible of the goal of a decent home and a suitable living environment for every American family, thus contributing to the development and redevelopment of communities and the advancement of the growth, wealth, and security of the Nation.[1]

The aims expressed in the Housing Act, then, heavily emphasize the elimination of substandard housing and the provision of better housing. The sections dealing with urban renewal are no less specific.

> . . . appropriate local public bodies shall be encouraged and assisted to undertake positive programs of encouraging and assisting the development of well-planned, integrated residential neighborhoods, the development and redevelopment of communities, and the production, at lower costs, of housing of sound standards of design, construction, livability, and size for adequate family life . . .[2]

Perhaps it is pretentious to speak of the assumptions that undergird the law as a "theory." Nevertheless, an effort at controlled social change must rest upon a belief, however incoherent, as to the nature of things and how they can be changed: It must also posit a desired condition as an achievable end. We shall look, then, at the ends desired by those who wrote the Housing Act, then at the constraints within which they must be achieved, and finally at the kinds of tools that are to be used in their achievement.

Although the chief emphasis in the law creating the Urban Renewal Agency is on housing, it does not stand alone in the statement of policy. In fact, the statement allows three levels of judgment: They approximate the aged trinity of "the good, the true, and the beautiful." The good is represented by a welfare aim, "a decent home and a suitable living environment for every American family"; the true is represented by the invocation of rational order, "well-planned, integrated residential neighborhoods"; while the beautiful seems covertly present in the phrases "of sound standards of *design*" and "the development and redevelopment of *communities*" (my

---

[1] The Housing Act of 1949, As Amended Through June, 1961 (Public Law 171, 81st Congress), Sec. 2.

[2] *Ibid.*, Sec. 3.

italics). Such terms are extraordinarily vague: They may all simply refer to better houses in better neighborhoods, or they may also encompass such goals as a rational location pattern for an entire metropolis and a "city beautiful," replete with monuments and parks. As we shall see, they have increasingly been interpreted in the latter sense by the Congress and the administrative branch.

These goals are to be attained, however, only within some rigid conditions.[3] The two most salient ones require that this program, though supported by the federal treasury and the police power, be brought into being in any locality only at the instigation of the local political structure ("appropriate *local* bodies shall be encouraged and assisted . . ."), and that it rely for actual construction of private use buildings (excepting public housing) upon the private market (*"private* enterprise shall be encouraged to serve as large a part of the total need as it can").[4] Underlying these provisos are basic norms, held widely by Americans, as to what the federal government should and should not do. It should not usurp the rights of localities, and it should not interfere with the right of private enterprise to exploit the market (especially, it might be noted, in real estate). Government should do, as the late Senator Taft was fond of remarking, "what the private market is unable to do." The requirement that local agencies initiate programs and that local communities contribute part of their costs is meant to assure both the free choice of the local community and its commitment to the program. The inability of urban renewal authorities to build assures a dependence on the private real estate industry.

Within these limits, what are to be the means for achieving these goals? At the highest level of generality, the Housing Act requires planning.

---

[3]Underlying any governmental program is the assumption that existing law and order will not be violated, and so many other conditions are assumed. I have only highlighted those that have basic consequences for the program *and that could, theoretically, have been differently defined.*

[4]Housing Act of 1949, As Amended Through June, 1961, Sec. 2 (my italics). The only other exception (besides public housing) is that local public facilities may be built by governmental bodies.

No contract shall be entered into for any loan or capital grant . . . unless (1) there is presented to the Administrator by the locality a workable program for community improvement (which shall include an official plan of action, as it exists from time to time, for effectively dealing with the establishment and preservation of a well-planned community with well-organized residential neighborhoods of decent homes and suitable living environment for adequate family life) for utilizing appropriate private and public resources to eliminate, and prevent the development or spread of, slums and urban blight, to encourage needed urban rehabilitation, to provide for the redevelopment of blighted, deteriorated, or slum areas, or to undertake such of the aforesaid activities or other feasible community activities as may be suitably employed to achieve the objective of such a program . . .[5]

This is extremely vague language. We shall see later how it has been administratively translated into the "Workable Program" requirement. For the rest it is enough to remember that *federal grants and loans are made contingent upon compliance with the Urban Renewal Agency's theories.* These are theories of (1) slum elimination and prevention, (2) rational urban location, and (3) proper community development.

Achievement Tools

The program can generate two basic kinds of leverage. First, and most spectacularly, it can be used to buy land through market negotiations or through forced purchase under the right of eminent domain. This land can then be cleared of structures and disposed of to new owners for specified kinds of development. Secondly, it can require that local governments pass and enforce ordinances respecting, for example, the maintenance and use of structures. Each of these requires a movement of policy from the federal program to the local public authority (LPA, as it is usually abbreviated). The American jealousy of local community rights supports this require-

[5] *Ibid,* Sec. 101, parens. (c).

ment; it is in the municipality, after all, that land is cleared and sold, that code violations are detected and corrected.

These tools are used differently for the three purposes of the program. Generalizing from the way the law is usually interpreted, the elimination and prevention of slums is to be brought about in this fashion. First, those structures that are so far gone that the cost of rehabilitating them would be greater than their final market value are destroyed. The land on which they stood is sold to other users, frequently for other uses. Secondly, through code enforcement those structures that are capable of rehabilitation are brought up to the specifications of the housing codes. Crowding, dilapidation, and inadequate sanitary facilities are remedied. As a net product, one will eliminate slums at a given time. A program of continuous enforcement should prevent their further development.

The promotion of a well-planned neighborhood is expanded to mean the development of well-planned cities, for the character of the neighborhood is due to its place in a larger system. And, since cities are already developed, this can only mean changing land uses. Here the achievement tools are used to change property ownership. Structures are razed, and the land is sold to new owners for new purposes; one then moves toward a situation that finds the right use in the right place, the right business on the right corner, the right people in the right neighborhood.

The development and redevelopment of the community is interpreted to mean the particular municipality in which the LPA is situated. Thus it usually means the central city of a metropolitan area and, within that city, the central business district (or CBD, as it is usually called). In creating the "city beautiful" at the center, the major tool is large-scale clearance and planned redevelopment, with the LPA using, wherever possible, architectural competitions to produce the most pleasant designs.

It is, then, with these three different goals and separate strategies that the urban renewal program is put in the field. But it is a long way from the aims of a federal document, no matter how legitimate it may be, to the specific action taken on *this* block in *this* city. It is wise to look briefly now at the organizational structure that is to translate this law, this set of "legitimatized aspirations," into living, concrete fact.

Organizational Structure

Urban renewal is a program that moves directly from an agency of the federal government to the municipality. Between the office in Washington and City Hall lies only the regional office, and the regional office functions chiefly as a monitor and processing point, implementing decisions ultimately made in Washington. Thus the program brings about one of the closest organizational ties between Washington and local municipal government that has ever existed.

The specific reasons for generating projects are as varied as the local political systems. In general, however, the "carrot" is the federal government's ability to take two-thirds of the cash loss involved in the process of buying land and "writing down" its value to what the market will bring. (There are also various kinds of minor grants, loans, and advances available, useful in piecing out the scanty fiscal powers of the municipality.) The projects, as noted earlier, are initiated at the local level. They must, however, be passed upon by the federal agency at a number of points. The first stage is in the granting of a "planning advance" to be used in working out the detailed plan specified in the legislation (cf., *supra,* footnote 5). The second stage of surveillance is the most crucial; it is the evaluation of the urban renewal plan by the national office which culminates in either an execution grant or the rejection of a plan. Finally, the agency exercises surveillance during the course of a project, through spot checks of relocated families, through independent assessments of property values, and through the acceptance or rejection of project costs, local contributions, and so forth.

Federal acceptance of a plan, leading to an execution grant for a project, requires that three kinds of evidence be supplied by the

LPA. First, the financial feasibility of a specific project must be demonstrated. Secondly, evidence of local political commitment, in the shape of a statement signed by the responsible head(s) of local government, must be presented to the agency. Finally, a "workable program to eliminate and prevent slums" in the city proposing the project must be judged acceptable by the federal agency.

The Workable Program

Because it is the chief technical instrument used in guaranteeing that urban renewal will lead to the elimination and prevention of slums, the Workable Program is worth discussion in some detail. It amounts to a series of seven requirements upon the locality: Each LPA must present evidence that it is indeed fulfilling these requirements. They are:

1. adequate codes and ordinances for structure and use, adequately enforced;
2. a comprehensive community plan for land use and public capital development;
3. neighborhood analysis for the determination of blight;
4. administrative organization adequate to an all-out attack on slums and blight;
5. a responsible program for relocation of displaced families;
6. citizen participation in the entire program;
7. adequate financial resources for carrying out (1) through (6) above.

In total, this amounts to an extremely strenuous set of demands upon the typical municipal government. According to the Program, however, each is indispensable. Together they spell out the logical implications of the strategy discussed earlier. The elimination of slums and blight requires the identification of target areas; adequate code enforcement; a program to relocate families so as to minimize the amount of social cost levied upon the poorest and to prevent other neighborhoods from overcrowding; and, at the same time, creates the fiscal and administrative resources for doing these things. Then too, prevention of future slums requires a plan for over-all land use while citizen participation is required (or thought to be required) if the program is not to die through lack of political support. It is, after all, a program sponsored by local elected political officials— no matter how much federal money is involved.

The Local Public Authority

George Duggar has given to the local urban renewal program the apt designation of "enterprise." Neither a bounded, centralized organization, nor a spontaneous expression of separate groups, it is a complex of agreements among groups that must go on over several years if the program is to have any results. LPAs may be subagencies of a city government, they may be combined with existing housing authorities, or they may be separate legal entities. In any case, they must have the active cooperation of a wide range of organizations and groups. It would be superfluous to list them all, but certain categories are basic. They include local political officials, potential redevelopers in the private real estate business, and the federal Urban Renewal Administration. The LPA reflects, vividly, the double commitments of the program: to local and federal polities and to public and private sectors of the economy.

The men who head these agencies are appointed officials of local governments. They are usually well-paid by governmental standards, but they often have no strong rights to tenure. They are, along with their key line officers, soldiers of local political fortune. Like the city managers, they hold their jobs by the will of the political leaders and, like them, they exercise such power and influence as they can generate through their multiple commitments and alliances. Their sources of support include the political leaders, other influential people in the community, and sources of "outside" money and professional recognition (including large redevelopment firms and the federal agency). The directors of the LPAs may be thought of as "public entrepreneurs."

This, then, is the formal structure of urban renewal as a program. Its charter spells out broad purposes—to eliminate slums from American cities, plan neighborhoods, and develop communities. It also confers great powers, including a substantial sum from the public treasury. But it works within certain radical limits: It must act only in cooperation with local municipal governments and the private real estate industry. Then, to protect the purposes of the program, the federal agency makes rigid requirements of the LPA that proposes a local action. These are rules of procedure backed up by the ability of the URA to refuse to certify a project as desirable, a "workable program" as acceptable; they can lead to a refusal to disburse public funds for the given project. Thus the public entrepreneurs at the local level must satisfy the requirements of their job through accommodating two sets of pressures—those from the local community and those from the federal agency.

This is not a simple or an easy task.

Chapter 2

URBAN RENEWAL AS A THEORY

The movement to clear the slums had its origins during the Great Depression of the 1930's. It rested upon accumulated dissatisfaction with some of the social consequences of city life, as well as the desire to get people to work, "builders to building, lenders to lending." Those who pressed for attention to such matters were not, however, slum dwellers themselves; they were self-selected members of middle-class society concerned with social welfare and the public interest. Such people try to represent both the interest of the poor and the society's interest in the consequences of urban slums. Ashworth speaks of English slums in the early nineteenth century:

> Their inhabitants were in no position to obtain the constitution of any additional (governing) body, and for a time no one from outside felt much interest in discovering what their problems were or, indeed, that they had any special problems of their own. But the societies of the new congested districts were not discrete entities and more and more people outside them gradually become aware of the pressure of their novel, powerful, and alarming qualities. Even if he were not his brother's keeper, every man of property was affected by the multiplication of thieves; everyone who valued his life felt it desirable not to have a mass of carriers of virulent diseases too close at hand. . . . It was morality (or, more exactly, criminality) and disease that were causing concern. Overcrowding and congestion, poverty,

crime, ill-health and heavy mortality were shown to be conditions found together.[1]

Concern with slums as centers of poverty, crime, and ill-health is still with us.

In America the accelerating growth of urban concentrations during the nineteenth century had also produced these enormous neighborhoods of the poor. Here, too, investigators and reformers began to define them as major urban problems. Some reformers even defined the city itself as the cause of evil and attempted to recapture the agrarian virtues—going so far as to export slum children to the hinterland.[2] In time, the effort changed toward the settlement house movement, the growth of private charities, and pressure for public aid. These efforts were illuminated by social surveys that defined the poor neighborhoods of the city as "problems"—and type-cast *places* as villains. Poverty, crime, disease, broken families, and the like were linked together in certain geographical areas of the city where housing was deteriorated and rents low; these neighborhoods were given the summary name, "the slums."

Slums were seen as threats to the larger society. As the centers of concentration for criminals and diseased persons, they were "contagious," for their effects were apt to spill over into the city as a whole. Then too, as aggregations of the most unfortunate, speaking foreign languages and living in different worlds, they were suspected as aliens, seditionists, and possibly anarchists. Some observers, like Jane Addams, considered the development of children in such environment as grounds for anxiety; what kind of equity was this—and what kind of new generation was being reared in the "city within a city," as Robert Park called it?

The complex interaction of poverty, the housing market, and the layout of the city were all lumped together in the term, slums. Poor

[1] William Ashworth, *The Genesis of Modern British Town Planning* (London: Routledge and Kegan Paul Ltd., 1954), pp. 47–48.

[2] Cf., Anselm Strauss, *Images of the American City* (New York: The Free Press of Glencoe, 1961), pp. 178–179. See also the discussion of rural values in urban America found in Robert Wood, *Suburbia* (Boston: Houghton-Mifflin Co., 1959).

people lived in certain houses on certain streets, mostly through necessity. And poor folks have poor ways. Yet these observations were combined and reified, and slums were thought of as things in themselves, having malignant powers and spreading like cancer. Buildings infected buildings and the latter, in turn, infected people. Thus the physical environment took on an overweening importance in the minds of reformers: Out of all the important consumer goods, *housing* became a major focus, for housing was considered the key to the elimination of slums.

The Program to Eliminate Slums: 1937

The New Deal launched many new programs aimed at achieving certain social goals immediately, as well as contributing to the long-run aim of "priming the pump" of the economy. One major goal was the improvement of housing, which resulted in the Housing Act of 1937. For those who could afford to buy or build if they could obtain money, this act provided help with mortgages; for those who could not afford decent housing, it provided public housing. Thus the first slum-clearance effort consisted simply of tearing down the offending slums and replacing them with publicly subsidized housing. The program had the anticipated effect of stimulating the construction industry and it eventually produced nearly three million public-housing units for the poor. In the process, an approximately equal number of dilapidated houses in crowded city neighborhoods was demolished. Tall public-housing apartment buildings took their place.

The program might be called, indifferently, public housing or slum clearance. Few public-housing units were ever built in the middle-class areas of the outer city because citizens protested vigorously at the threat of public housing nearby; they were built on the site of slums. Then, as housing became more plentiful, public housing became increasingly a service for the bottom dogs—broken families, the aged poor, the ill, and, especially, residentially restricted Negroes. Objections to public housing now combined distaste for Negroes with distaste for the poor as neighbors. As a result of citizen pressure on local politicians, public housing was more and more often sited in the center of the Negro districts and, to avoid a net decrease in available housing, the structures grew taller.[3]

This public housing has been called, with some justice, "minimal charity." Those with no choice were housed in apartments high up in tall buildings, in the center of the city. This was the exact opposite of the housing preferred by Americans who had a choice—the single family unit surrounded by its own yard, convenient for the surveillance of children and offering a degree of privacy. Public housing was operated by managers who carried over criteria of the real estate business to what was essentially a welfare program, men whose pride was in high collection rates and low vacancies, low breakage and minimal costs. These are all useful rules for real estate management no doubt; they are not so relevant to the problems of maintaining order, safety, and community among the concentrated mass of the poor who make up public housing's clientele.

Thus, as typical public housing became slab towers filled with poor Negroes in the middle of Negro working-class neighborhoods, it developed its own critics among the liberals who once fought for it. They spoke of it as "immuring the slums," or "slums with hot running water."[4] Some spoke of it as a way of increasing segregation in the slums. As the social climate of the Depression evaporated in the economic sun of the postwar years, the program steadily lost popularity.

[3]Martin Meyerson and Edward C. Banfield, *Politics, Planning, and the Public Interest* (Glencoe: The Free Press, 1955), describe in convincing detail the struggle over public-housing sites in Chicago.

[4]See, for example, Jane Jacobs, *The Death and Life of Great American Cities* (New York: Random House, 1961); also Catherine Bauer, "The Dreary Deadlock in Public Housing," *Architectural Forum*, CVI (May 1957), 140–142, 219–222.

Urban Redevelopment: 1949

Disenchantment with the public-housing kind of slum clearance was caused by more than its unpopularity as a housing program. It was becoming clear that, at the then current rate of development, public housing could never rebuild all the neighborhoods that had deteriorated during the decade of the Depression and five years of war. And, in the post-Depression climate of thought, continued large-scale investment in public works did not appear politically unpopular. Thus a bipartisan coalition developed the legislation that eventually became the Taft-Ellender-Wagner Bill, the Housing Act of 1949. A portfolio bill including provisions for public housing and mortgage insurance as well, it provided the basic charter for urban redevelopment.

This bill was a center of controversy for several years before its enactment.[5] It was felt to be popular because of the severe housing shortage resulting from depression and war. On the other hand, "Objections to the comprehensive housing legislation as a whole, and particularly bitter objections to the public housing provisions, were expressed by every national trade organization whose members were primarily engaged in producing, financing, or dealing with residential property."[6] Foard and Fefferman believe that the public housing provision acted as a stalking horse for urban redevelopment: In the intensity of opposition to public housing, the program to clear land and sell it on the market escaped radical censure. As one conservative critic put it, "I am in favor of the slum elimination section. I am opposed to the public housing section."[7] This schism between the support for public housing and that for urban development continues

---

[5]See the excellent brief history of urban renewal law in Ashley A. Foard and Hilbert Fefferman, "Federal Urban Renewal Legislation," *Law and Contemporary Politics*, Vol. 25, No. 4 (Autumn 1960), pp. 635–684.

[6]*Ibid.*, p. 650.

[7]Senator John Bricker, quoted in *ibid.*, p. 648.

to the present, and is one of the important horns in several dilemmas.

The new program was popular with a wide range of supporters, and those concerned with rebuilding the cities had high hopes for it. The bill was still primarily focused upon housing and the neighborhood, however, and required that any area redeveloped should be predominantly residential—that is, over half the acreage should be devoted to residential uses. As the Taft subcommittee report put it: "The Subcommittee is not convinced that the federal government should embark upon a general program of aid to cities looking to their rebuilding in more attractive and economical patterns."[8]

Senator Taft argued that the over-all structure of the urban areas should be taken as given. The program should be aimed at a constant improvement of housing within the existing layout of cities—a concentration upon "spot removal." The planners, with whom he argued in the hearings on the bill, tended to see "spots" as symptoms of the larger system. This dichotomy runs throughout the history of the urban renewal program.

Urban Renewal: 1954

The urban redevelopment program created by the 1949 Housing Act was criticized on several counts. Many were distressed at the problems created for the very poor who were displaced by projects in a time of severe housing shortage. Others pointed out the impossibility of financing over-all redevelopment, when evidence accumulated to show that "blight" was growing faster than redevelopment. The weakness of housing codes and their enforcement seemed to some an obvious contributory factor in the problem; the continued unplanned development of cities bothered others. In response to a wide range of criticisms, the Housing Act of 1949 was amended in 1954 with support from a bipartisan coalition and a Republican administration.

---

[8]Quoted in Foard and Fefferman, "Legislation," p. 663.

The major innovation in redevelopment was the Workable Program. As described earlier, it is a logical answer to many, if not all, of the Acts' criticisms. It was so written as to increase the contributions of private enterprise, the responsibility of local government, and the participation of private citizens in the neighborhoods to be conserved or rehabilitated. In sum, these changes were expected to produce more results with fewer federal dollars. The amendments allocated funds for more public housing, needed for the displaced, but they also allowed the use of 10 per cent of grants-in-aid for areas not primarily residential or not to be redeveloped as residential. The overwhelming emphasis upon housing was moderated for the first time.

The slum clearance programs of 1937 had evolved into the urban renewal program of 1954. The program was now focused upon much more than the redevelopment of deteriorated neighborhoods; it was assigned the task of conserving the existing stock of housing, rehabilitating that which was beginning to deteriorate, and planning that which was to be built. It was to result in the clarification and enforcement of housing standards as statutory acts. Cities had to be planned in a comprehensive fashion, nonresidential areas redeveloped, rehabilitated, or conserved, and the private real estate market controlled through indirection.

The planners won with a vengeance, and Senator Taft lost. If "slums and blight" are but symptoms of a larger whole, whoever defines that whole and its proper nature is defining the program. The Housing Act was further amended in 1961; again the emphasis was upon nonresidential redevelopment. The percentage allowed was extended to 30 per cent, while the major intellectual innovation was the provision for a comprehensive renewal program, to encompass the entire city in one plan for the future.

The reader has probably noticed how few definitions have been given. This is partly because in the universe of discourse definitions are very rare, and partly because the problem is so basic to an understanding of the way urban renewal is practiced that it deserves systematic discussion.

Definitions, Arguments, and Measures: The Bones of Theory

A blueprint for social action can be broken down usefully into three kinds of components. First, there are *definitions* that are used to identify the important elements in the situation to be changed and the useful tools for changing it. Secondly, there are ideas about *cause* used to explain the existence of the problem, and thus the conditions for changing it. These are linked together in arguments that support the use of some given treatment for a given problem. Finally, and very important, there are _measurement_ concepts, used to translate the definitions (of problem and of treatment) into precise identifications in a concrete situation. The importance of these measurement concepts lies in the actor's practical dependence upon them. In practice the definition gets simplified to *whatever the measurements measure.*[9]

The most important definitional concept used in the urban renewal program is that of "slums or blighted areas." When one reads the legislation to find the target of the program, the phase turns up repeatedly; it is the key term in the program's *raison d'être.* Yet nowhere in the law is the phrase defined. In the Declaration of National Housing Policy we are told that the purpose of the act is "the elimination of substandard *and other inadequate* housing," and "the goal of a decent home and a *suitable* living environment for every American family" [my italics].

Such lack of definition is not unusual in the law. It is to be expected whenever a term or phrase is so widely known and has such a standard connotation and denotation that all will agree on its

[9]For example, if one's measure of intelligence is a child's response to a Stanford-Binet intelligence test, the child's IQ score, for practical purposes, is his intelligence: All that is not measured by the test is irrelevant to decision. No concepts are more important than those we use for identification and measure of the world. For a lengthy discussion of this matter, see Aaron Cicourel, *Method and Measurement in Sociology* (New York: The Free Press of Glencoe, 1964).

meaning. This, however, is far from true where the words "slum" and "blight," are concerned. Allen A. Twichell, in charge of the American Public Health Association's work in formulating housing standards and measures, has this to say about blight:

> It usually refers to an area or district of some size. It refers to no one characteristic or condition, nor even to any one set of conditions or characteristics that are always found in the same combination. Instead, it covers a fairly wide range of conditions and characteristics that from example to example are found in differing combinations, and with or without certain secondary features.[10]

Such a definition is extremely difficult to apply, since it cannot specify necessary and sufficient conditions for proving that blight exists. There is a considerable likelihood that the terms "blight" and "nonblight" will not be mutually exclusive. Thus, one man's blight may be another man's nonblight, depending upon how important he thinks a given condition or characteristic to be. Yet people's homes are condemned and destroyed because they fall in the blight category, and billions of dollars are spent in blight removal. The problem is a crucial one; it is no less than that of defining the official norms of housing in American society. How is the term "decent" to be changed from a subjective reaction to one that is objective, one that can be consistently applied and, therefore, allow an equitable public policy? A just policy cannot be based upon a rubber measuring stick, for then the law would not apply equally to all.

As we have noted, the term "slum" was applied to areas where certain people and structures were concentrated. As Ashworth notes, these areas were defined as problems of the public because criminality and disease were widespread among their residents. The general meaning of slums has not changed much since 1842: Slums are neighborhoods where the "social pathologies" of alcoholism, dis-

---

[10]"Measuring the Quality of Housing," in *Urban Redevelopment; Problems and Practices,* ed. Coleman Woodbury (Chicago: University of Chicago Press, 1953), p. 11.

ordered family life, prostitution, and the like, are common occur-
rences. In addition, slums are neighborhoods with given structural
characteristics. They are old, the houses are esthetically displeasing
to the slum definer, the rents are relatively low, the houses are
crowded. Since the two kinds of attributes—the social and the
physical—coexist in given areas, the attack of public policy on slums
has been implemented in the Housing Act. But in that Act the
negative, "slums," is vague, and it is accompanied by an equally
vague positive, "decent homes."

Decent homes are whatever structures are acceptable among the
relevant social group. Standards vary greatly. Sergei Grimm, the
planner, tells of his determination to find out what "substandard"
meant to the man on the street. After a certain amount of question-
ing, he reported, "I found out. Substandard is whatever is worst *in
our neighborhood!*" [11] Decency is an open-ended definition: As con-
sumption norms move upward and the average aspiration for housing moves with them, a proportion of houses built to earlier design
becomes "indecent." The open-ended definition of good neighborhoods allows an open-ended definition of slums.

The government, to implement its program for slum elimination
and prevention, must define decent housing. But "decent" is a value
judgment, and it cannot be a definition which is empirically and
logically coercive. "Blight" is not just an aspect of things; it is also a
judgment of them. Where such a situation holds, agreement is not
possible through investigation and test; it is produced by persuasion
and compliance. The concept of blight is translated into fact by fiat.

This crucial judgment results then from the application of administratively framed housing standards. Twichell resolves the problem
in these terms: "Without trying to make this definition too fine, it
would probably be agreed that the two basic characteristics of
blighted areas are substandardness and either stagnation or deterioration." But these two notions are really one, for "stagnation or deterioration" is defined by progressive "substandardness."

[11]In personal communication.

In the past, once districts have started downhill (i.e., *have begun to fall below minimum standards,* either because of physical or economic change in the district itself or in its vicinity *or because the standards have risen* over a period of time), most of them have continued downward and often at an increasing rate.[12] [Italics mine.]

Whoever is framing the housing code, then, is creating "blighted areas" by definition. If "standards have risen," in Twichell's terms, an area goes "downhill."

There are several "model" housing codes in general use. One is that of the American Public Health Association, created by Mr. Twichell; another is the Uniform Housing Code, developed in the San Francisco Bay Area and required for the acceptable Workable Program in western cities. The codes spell out minimally acceptable space and occupancy standards, light and ventilation, sanitation, heating, electrical, and structural conditions. The codes spell out a type of housing that is modest by American standards, though wildly utopian for most of the remainder of humanity. They include the all-American bathroom, hot running water, and other amenities of middle-class, urban life. The codes have been very influential and their influence has been increased by the Workable Program requirement, for the Urban Renewal Administration has the power to judge codes for "acceptability."

Nevertheless, the arbitrary nature of the codes is clear from a comparison of those enacted by different cities.[13] Of fifty-six cities listed in one study, fifteen had no requirements for minimal space, and in the other forty-one cities, it ranged from fifty to one hundred square feet per occupant; most cities had requirements for light and ventilation, but they ranged from 6 per cent of the wall area in Norfolk to 12½ per cent in Los Angeles; similarly, only four persons might share a water-closet in Denver, but twenty might do so in Los Angeles, and there was no limit in Baltimore. The same variation occurred with

[12]Twichell, in Woodbury, *op. cit.,* pp. 11–12.
[13]*Provisions of Housing Codes in Various American Cities* (Washington, D.C.; Housing and Home Finance Agency, Urban Renewal Administration, 1956). The codes are probably becoming more uniform as a result of pressure from the URA.

every requirement of the codes. Decent housing was not uniformly defined, even among housing officials of large American cities.

A slum or blighted area is, for purposes of urban renewal, an areally concentrated collection of substandard dwellings. This administrative definition does not say anything at all about the causes of such conditions. Causal theory is important, however, for action aimed at changing them. Looking at the literature on the subject, including the technical bulletins of the URA, one can only conclude that "blight" is thought of as a social disease. Thus:

> Blight does not stand still. It has a way of spreading from house to house, from block to block, from neighborhood to neighborhood.
> Caught early enough, blight can be arrested and the downward trend reversed. On the other hand, once an area has reached an advanced stage of deterioration, nothing short of the major surgery of clearance and redevelopment will suffice. Start to work now on the areas in the early stages of blight that have strength and vitality enough to enable them to respond to the preventative and corrective therapy of conservation.[14]

However, at a more mundane level, blight is due to either (1) substandardness in original construction, (2) lack of maintenance, or (3) a substandard use—i.e., crowding and the like. The first case reflects either a discrepancy in housing norms between builder and code-writer or a change in standards over time; the second reflects lack of capital investment; the third usually indicates a different use of the building than that originally planned.

As William Grigsby has recently remarked, the naive belief is that most substandardness is produced by lack of maintenance.[15] Lack of maintenance is, then, assumed to flow from lack of commitment to either the house or the neighborhood. (In the technical guide quoted in footnote[14], administrators are advised to choose areas in which most homes are owned, in districts that people like.) This emphasis

---

[14]*Selecting Areas for Conservation*, Urban Renewal Service Technical Guide 3 (Washington, D.C.: Urban Renewal Administration, September 1960), p. 1.

[15]William Grigsby, *Housing Markets and Public Policy* (Philadelphia: University of Pennsylvania Press, 1964), p. 229. In fact, some two-thirds is due to plumbing, reflecting in most cases the standards used in original construction.

upon maintenance as the key to substandardness results in a tripartite classification of problem areas. First, there are the "rock bottom slums," adjudged to be so far gone in substandardness that nobody would want to rehabilitate them; here clearance is required. Secondly, there are neighborhoods which can be "spot redeveloped" and rehabilitated through code enforcement and the private action of owners. Thirdly, there are the neighborhoods that are judged "basically sound," requiring only increased capital input by the owners in the form of renovation and better maintenance. The first areas are called *clearance areas,* the second *rehabilitation areas,* the third, *conservation areas.* They are defined, basically, by the proportion of units which are substandard and the probable individual cost of bringing the units up to code requirements. If the cost is so high as to represent a poor investment (if it is greater than the market value of the house will be after rehabilitation) it is judged fit only for demolition.

Thus the maintenance and improvement of the *existing* housing stock is a basic aim of urban renewal. The reasoning behind this emphasis upon the existing stock is very simple:

> Existing dwellings constitute the greatest housing resource at our disposal. It is this supply of older housing that must be preserved if we are to meet the housing requirements of the large segment of the American people who cannot afford, or do not desire, new housing. . . .
>
> Our cities cannot be renewed nor blight eliminated and potential blight arrested by clearance and redevelopment alone. Only by utilizing conservation and rehabilitation as well as clearance can we be successful. . . .[16]

And, since substandard houses tend to cluster by area, substandard *areas* are the focus of efforts at rehabilitation and conservation. Such areas are defined by their present conditions and by the possibility of their being upgraded at the cost of the owners. How is this to be done?

The Workable Program for the elimination and prevention of slums is based on certain assumptions about how people can be con-

[16]*Home Improvement,* Bulletin 2, Urban Renewal Service (Washington, D.C.: Urban Renewal Administration, October 1960).

trolled. It will work only if those assumptions hold. Those assumptions may be grouped around the various subgoals of the program: (1) the destruction of existing slums and their replacement with standard structures, (2) the rehousing of ex-slum dwellers in standard housing, (3) the enforcement of housing codes so as to bring existing houses up to code standards, and, (4) the use of the local capital budget to improve public facilities in substandard areas.

Clearance of existing slums and replacement.   One must assume that local governmental officials will designate "rock bottom slum" areas for projects, that the local political process will allow this designation (i.e., slum dwellers and owners will comply), and that private real estate interests will bid for the land and build standard dwellings on it.

Re-housing of ex-slum dwellers in standard housing.   One must assume that a supply of such housing exists at a price the slum dwellers can and will afford to pay; that they have knowledge of such housing; that they are willing and able to move into it.

The enforcing of housing codes.   One must assume that the codes do indeed define "non-slum" housing individually and in the spatial aggregate, that local governmental officials can and will apply the same measure to all areas alike, that the owners of structures can be forced (or persuaded) to comply with the code requirements, and that this can be done rapidly enough to bring about a net decrease in number of substandard dwellings.

The use of local capital budget.   One must assume that capital improvements in public services will improve the "decency" of neighborhoods, that local officials will allocate larger resources to the substandard areas, that the local political process will support such increased use of tax money, and that this will occur at a pace that is related to the general private improvement of dwelling units.

These assumptions are all questionable. The present substandard use of a space is no guarantee that it has attractions on the private land market: Substandard use would create a presumption to the contrary. Nor does the fact that given populations now live in slums necessarily indicate any overriding desire to live in standard housing and standard neighborhoods. Insofar as self-selection was involved in their original choice, it would presumably still operate. Those who choose other consumer goods over more expensive housing would still do so. The dubious quality of housing as defined by local codes has led to administrative control from URA; nevertheless, the assumption that codes can be enforced against the will of the population requires that we ignore the role of the coerced citizens as voters and taxpayers. Finally, urban renewal is a federal program largely because of the fiscal straits of the municipalities; this argues a very moderate increase in public capital investment for the neighborhoods inhabited by the poorest and politically least effective citizens.

However, the Urban Renewal Administration has very weak tools for testing the degree to which the assumptions indeed hold. The Workable Program is a document summarizing local actions taken in each category prescribed. This document is prepared by the LPA and is rarely based upon adequate information. Many relocatees are "lost"; little is known about the quality of code enforcement; alternative sites for redevelopment are rarely discussed; the over-all use of public capital budget is not critically evaluated in terms of the commitment presumably made by the municipality. In short, a document of good intentions is substituted for other measures of the program. The next chapter shows that there are good administrative reasons for using this particular "measure" to determine compliance with the Program.

The Augmented Program: 1961

The Workable Program was never popular with most LPA officials. Its emphasis upon housing and relocation together forced a commitment to public housing. Its emphasis on code enforcement led agencies into very complex and emotion-generating public policy. And, as housing became in many cities a problem chiefly among Negroes, support for housing programs in general dwindled. At the same time, other interests pressed for more concern with the problems of the central business district of the city. The central city mayors were worried about tax bases, for, as downtown property declined, shopping centers grew by leaps and bounds in the suburbs. The mayors pressed for general programs of city redevelopment and for smaller local contributions to the program. Arguing that the local tax base is inadequate and regressive, the United States Conference of Mayors lobbied for an increase of the federal contribution from 66⅔ per cent to 80 per cent.[17] They were joined by influential allies; as Foard and Fefferman said in 1960:

> Foremost among these are department store owners and mortgage and other lenders concerned about large outstanding investments in downtown retail properties now suffering competition from suburban shopping centers. Redevelopment to provide downtown commercial centers with parking space and attractive surroundings is a business necessity to them and a source of increased tax revenue to the city.[18]

To these interests was joined the steady pressure of those theorists who had always felt that urban renewal should be concerned with the entire urban structure, that slums and blight are merely symptoms of weakness in the general pattern. For the directors of the various LPAs, such a change in orientation meant divorce from the unpopular issue of housing and an opportunity to enlist wide support for a program of community redevelopment. The propaganda of the deed is important to a new and unestablished program: What better propaganda was possible than the creation of new malls and tall towers in the CBD? The "city beautiful" appeals to the general public; a changed locational order, encouraging the "city profitable," appeals to downtown businessmen.

The mayors did not get their increased federal contribution. However, increasing laxness in the interpretation of public capital improvements as local contributions means that the local cash contribution has now shrunk to approximately 14 per cent.[19] They did get an increase in the nonresidential allowance, to 30 per cent of total

[17]Foard and Fefferman, "Legislation," p. 675. Some mayors wanted the federal government to pay 90 per cent.
[18]*Ibid.*, p. 672.
[19]*Ibid.*, p. 683.

grant funds. (This is approximately half again the percentage of the total urban area devoted to commercial uses.) When one remembers that 49 per cent of "predominantly residential" can be in truth non-residential, it is clear that as much as 64 per cent of the program can be devoted to improving nonresidential properties in a city. The planners got a provision for the development of total "community renewal programs," looking toward an integrated drive to rebuild and shape the entire central city.

Definitional Problems: Slums vs. Blight

We have been discussing slums and blight as though they were identical. As long as the program was limited to predominantly residential redevelopment, this identification was approximately correct. Today, with that "general program of aid to cities" which the Taft subcommittee deplored, "blight" has become the key term. Slums are merely "residential blight." The meaning of blight is not nearly as clear, even, as that of slums. Following Twichell, we can speak of it as substandard quality of structures—but "sub" what standard?

When a given space within a city is used for a given purpose —parking lot, City Hall, department store, factory—how does one determine if it is properly used? Again, the only standard possible is an administratively determined one, producing facts by fiat. In a recent and influential text on planning, for example, one author has this to say about blight:

> *Simple forms of blight* include such physical characteristics as structural deterioration, missing sanitation facilities, structures in disrepair or lacking in elemental maintenance, presence of trash and rubbish accumulations in yards, adverse environmental influences such as noise, odors, dust, and so on, and missing community facilities such as schools, playgrounds, public water and sewerage systems, and adequate street and drainage facilities. Usually associated with simple forms of physical blight are certain social and economic indicators of blight. Social indicators of blight include presence of abnormally high rates of juvenile delinquency, venereal disease, and similar results from other health and welfare indices; and economic indica-

tors include concentrations of tax delinquent and tax title properties, declining property values, and presence of an abnormally large number of
building vacancies. *Complex forms of blight* are said to exist when an area con-
tains a mixture of incompatible land uses (the classic illustration being the
glue factory located in the residential area), obsolete or impractical layout of
lots, blocks, and streets, unsafe and unhealthful conditions existing or possible when marginal land is in use, particularly land subject to floods,
marshiness, or tidal flows.[20]

Most of these indicators are quite irrelevant to any given area. Some
are, in fact, inevitable if an area has industrial or commercial activities. Blight, like slums, represents the parts of town that the observer
finds distasteful, but in even more different ways.

The measures actually used for nonresidential neighborhoods are
those listed as economic indicators—tax delinquency, declining
property values, and vacancies. They are usually held to occur
because of the conditions that Chapin terms "complex blight." Because of mixed land uses, obsolete street layouts, and drainage
problems, the area is economically less productive: The deterioration
of trade and therefore of economic value results. And as this occurs,
the present occupiers of the land use it in such a way that private
redevelopment is discouraged.[21]

Many areas in any city are slowly losing their competitive value
on the land market. How, then, is one to determine which areas are
the truly blighted ones? Chapin's definition is of no use, for given
attributes may or may not occur in given instances. After all, a given
space may have value *only* for its present use: Hoover and Vernon
have documented the case for the economic necessity and value of
deteriorated commercial areas in cities. They see them as economically necessary for small, struggling enterprises, which include new
starts—they are venture capital for innovations.[22] There must be

[20]F. Stuart Chapin, Jr., *Urban Land Use Planning* (New York: Harper and Brothers,
1957), pp. 232–233.

[21]I have telescoped a long argument into a few propositions, chiefly because it is, intellectually, this simple. There is a large literature on urban real estate dealing with the
subject.

[22]Edgar M. Hoover and Raymond Vernon, *Anatomy of a Metropolis* (Cambridge:
Harvard University Press, 1959), especially Chap. 2.

cheap quarters for small businesses and they are apt to have higher vacancy rates and more tax delinquencies. There must be residential neighborhoods for the poor—they are bound to be largely made up of obsolete structures, indecent by a newer building code. In short, the "blighting" of urban areas is a logical product of a free market in land.

However, there is a criterion for the blighted area as against the simply cheap area. That is whether or not it could be rebuilt for a "higher" use. And by a higher use is almost always meant a more profitable use—one that increases tax assessments, increases the number and wealth of consumers in the neighborhood, and increases the profits of those with a stake in the CBD. Rents and taxes go up and vacancies down, as use becomes higher. The definition of blight is, simply, that "this land is too good for these people."

As urban renewal became a program to increase the goodness, truth, and beauty of the urban capital plant, residential and nonresidential alike, blight became an ever-expandable term. Like slums, it is an open-ended value judgment, based upon an open-ended aspiration for the given city. Any area might be judged by someone to deserve a "higher use." One who cares for parks might consider open space a higher use than the Empire State Building. But the economic criterion is crucial because of the program's basic commitment to the private real estate industry. Only that land that can be redeveloped at a profit will be bidden for—and only that which is bidden for can be raised to higher uses. The augmented Housing Act of 1961 put the municipalities and the URA squarely in the local downtown real estate market, as buyers, sellers, and speculators.

Renovation of the CBD

Thus urban renewal, though embedded in the Housing Act, with a purpose said to be the elimination and prevention of slums, is also a program for the renovation of the central business district. Enormous investments are being made in the purchase and clearance of downtown property; land cleared to date has been about 85 per cent residential, but most of it is then redeveloped as commercial facilities, office buildings, or expensive high-rise apartments. Certain assumptions are implicit in such a program.

1. It is assumed that the age and deterioration of structures produces lack of financial profitability and not vice versa. As a corollary, it is assumed that there is a large, untapped demand for CBD location among those who can afford high rentals and construction costs.

2. It is assumed that residential deterioration does not affect commercial development seriously, or that commercial redevelopment of the CBD can decrease deterioration in residential neighborhoods of the central city.

These assumptions are necessary. The first one is required because, if demand for downtown land is constant or shrinking, the development of new structures can only lead to vacancies, lower rental, and eventual tax delinquency in those which remain—in short, blight. The second assumption is required if the program does not give major and effective attention to slum elimination. It is precisely around the CBD that the most deteriorated neighborhoods now stand, and the progressive destruction of low-income housing without a complementary increase in standard low-cost housing can only shift the slums from one location to another. If the nearby existence of large substandard areas, inhabited by poor Negroes, hurts the commercial profitability of the CBD, then *commercial* redevelopment alone is no solution.

In summary, the slum clearance provisions of the Housing Act of 1937 have been slowly transformed into a large-scale program to redevelop the central city. In the process, the vague term "slum" has been subsumed under the vaguer term "blight." In this discussion, for clarity's sake, slum refers to the poor housing in which live the poor members of the society, and blight refers to a land use that is not as profitable as some alternative, in terms of general values, usually financial.

One might simplify and say: "Slum elimination requires that the housing of the poor be improved; blight elimination necessitates the

movement of the right activities to the right location." Slum elimination and prevention does not make necessary any great shift in
business and industrial plants or any commercial rebirth of the CBD.
It does not require a better transportation system and location grid
for the city in terms of efficiency, beauty, or civic pride. Contrari-
wise, the elimination of blight does not require the elimination of the
poor housing of the poor; it simply means it must be located in the
right place. That might very well be exactly where it is now located,
given the cost to the society of acquiring the land from its present owners
and writing it down to the value bidders assign it.[23]

The aims of the program are now extremely global; they are not
necessarily contradictory: If the displaced poor are relocated in improved housing, if neighborhoods are maintained or upgraded, if
better housing in better locations is available for all, the CBD may
also be replanned and redeveloped without contradiction. However,
the aims of slum elimination and blight elimination, as the terms are
used here, are most certainly not identical. And, given scarce resources, to choose one is to reject the other in that degree.

There is, then, a problem of priorities. First, one must decide the
relative importance of blight removal as against slum clearance.
Secondly, within each kind of program one must decide where the
action will occur. Out of all of the neighborhoods of the poor, which
will be rehabilitated or redeveloped? Out of all the declining commercial and industrial areas, which will be selected for a project? How
do you estimate, before commitment, the general value of a project
in terms of removing slums forever, or removing generalized blight
forever? The Community Renewal Programs now being developed
are an effort to narrow alternatives, but such programs typically require so much action in so many places over so long a period of time
that they do not yield priorities. And, in truth, too little is known about
the causation of slums and blight for anyone to plan their elimina-

[23]This point is central to the analysis by Otis A. Davis and Andrew B. Whinston in
"The Economics of Urban Renewal," *Law and Contemporary Problems,* Vol. 26, No. 1
(Winter 1961), pp. 105 ff.

tion over a period of decades. The plans are at best informed guesses; at worst, they are efforts in a peculiar art form.

In the absence of an objective standard of priorities, the political process and the real estate market are the sources of a program's logic. The political response is a measure of its success. The LPAs move toward a program of downtown redevelopment and the upgrading of residential districts nearby because this is effective propaganda of the deed. They produce the positive response of relevant publics, including the political officials of the central city and the downtown businessmen. As it succeeds in this sense, it tends to set the precedent for other programs, in this and other cities. In the center of the city many persons can see the program's effects; and they are influential persons. Tall towers and green malls have a disproportionate intellectual appeal because of their esthetic effect. Meanwhile, most of the substandard houses, neighborhoods, and districts may remain exactly what they were before—substandard.

Chapter 3

URBAN RENEWAL AND THE
LOCAL COMMUNITY

Organizationally, the urban renewal program is one of the most complex ever attempted in the United States. It brings together in one harness, as semi-independent parties, the federal government and the local city council, various departments within City Hall (code inspection and enforcement, assessment, capital investment, public housing, land-use planning and zoning, and so forth), as well as different levels of local government (state, municipality, county, school district). Of equal importance, it requires the cooperation of private citizens; as residents in the neighborhoods, owners of property to be redeveloped, voters in referenda on bond issues, and investors in the real estate market.

All of these are to be coordinated in a program that violates many accepted normative distinctions of American society. The methods are unusual for local government. Lines between public and private (originally drawn to prevent collusion and corruption) are blurred. Private market activity is to be judged by its effect on public uses; public development has as its goal private uses. The aim of the enterprise is no less than radical: It is to reverse partially the American definition of property rights. For the blight of the cities results from either lack of maintenance or failure to redevelop land upon the change of its use-value in the city. These omissions were possible because of the strong presumption that the owner has the right to determine land use. Though there have been laws for maintenance and planning on the books in some cities for some time, these laws have not affected action because of the weakness in the legal structures for enforcement and the weakness of local political structures in taking action that was rational for the interests of the community as a whole. But such a failure of law usually reflects the weakness of moral justification, because of a confusion as to just what the norms should be. Such moral confusion underlies our inability to plan and to enforce codes.

These conditions must be changed if the enterprise called urban renewal is to succeed. In understanding the possibilities and the limits of such change, it is useful to look at the program from the point of view of the local public authority, for here in the given city, where the land is taken and resold, all the lines come to focus.

George Duggar has spoken of the LPA as an "enterprise": "An enterprise is defined as an undertaking in which formally independent organizations participate, none of which exerts authority crucial for the participation of the others. . . . The relationship is not flagrantly coercive at any link in the chain binding central to state, state to local government, or local government to local corporate authority (LPA)."[1] Because the relationship is not coercive, there is a demand upon the public enterpriser for reciprocity. He must give in order to receive. He must "coopt" many organizations for his purposes, but in the process he can expect to be coopted for the purposes of others.[2] Such cooptation, in turn, is crucial for the emerging goals of the enterprise. Though the formal aims of the LPA may remain "the elimination and prevention of slums and blight," the ground for consensus may be another thing.

The problems of the LPA director may be traced to the pressures

[1]George S. Duggar, "The Federal Concept in Urban Renewal: The Local Renewal Enterprise," *Community Development in the Western Hemisphere* (San Diego, California: Public Affairs Research Institute of San Diego College, August 1961), p. 41.
[2]Cf., Philip Selznick, *TVA and the Grassroots* (Berkeley and Los Angeles: University of California Press, 1949), for a discussion of cooptation.

upon him, but these in turn result from the necessary commitments that he must make in order to stay in business. Each pressure results from the problems of some group necessary to his enterprise. An irreducible list would include (1) the rank and file citizens and their political "opinion leaders," (2) the officials in the governmental agencies in his city, (3) business interests concerned with land use, and (4) the federal Urban Renewal Administration.

Rank and File Citizens and Their Leaders

The money for the local contribution to a program comes from the citizens. It is also their neighborhoods that are razed and their houses that are inspected and forced "up to code." The American norms of local autonomy and direct democracy mean that no local program can go on indefinitely if it does not have support at the polls from a majority of those who vote. Yet David A. Wallace has recently stated that, in his opinion: "By and large, people don't understand what we're after—or even what we're talking about. This is fortunate, for if they did, we'd all have to run for cover."[3] And one URA official remarked in an interview; "If we had to go to a referendum for all the programs, we might as well shut up shop tomorrow."

There is little information available with which one would measure the popular approval of the program, or even its general familiarity. In New Haven, Mayor Lee and his advisers took his startling success at the polls as a popular plebiscite on the New Haven program; in Boston, Mayor Collins pinned his political future on it. However, the defeat of Newark's Mayor Carlin is attributed to urban renewal by some, while bond issues for funds have recently been defeated in Chicago, St. Louis, Spokane (Washington), Eugene (Oregon), and a number of other cities.

In one small western city, Robert E. Agger and Bert Swanson dis-

---

[3]David A. Wallace "Beggars on Horseback," in *Ends and Means of Urban Renewal* (Philadelphia: Philadelphia Housing Association, 1961), p. 47.

covered that 38 per cent of a random sample approved of urban renewal, 11 per cent disapproved, and the remainder didn't care or didn't know. Eighty per cent of the *civic leaders* approved of the local program, but it was defeated decisively in a referendum.[4] This is a biased sample in that (1) there was an intensive campaign, pro and con the issue at the time, and (2) this was a small, university city, with almost 40 per cent of the nonstudent population having been to college.

More relevant is a sample survey conducted in a large western metropolis. The summary of the study states, in part:

> The words—"Urban Renewal"—have not yet reached or registered an impression on a majority of (inhabitants).
>
> While there are signs of a growing consciousness of Urban Renewal, tangible knowledge of the program is presently limited to one-fourth of the public. "Urban Renewal" is a completely new term to approximately half the community.
>
> In addition to lack of information, there is some misinformation on the subject. The main misconception is that Urban Renewal is related to, or a program for, *suburban* or outlying areas.

When the program was explained to the voters, 80 per cent approved, but when they realized government funds would be used for development projects, the margin shrank to 48 per cent approving versus 38 per cent opposed. The three most acceptable slogans were based on the "Perk Up Our City" theme, the stimulus of the program to local industry and the success of urban renewal in other cities.

Philadelphia has one of the largest, best publicized, and most successful urban renewal programs. Yet a recent study indicates how few people in the neighborhoods most likely to be targets for rehabilitation or clearance understand what it is all about. In West Philadelphia, an area in which major renewal is underway and massive

---

[4]Agger and Swanson, "The Politics of Urban Renewal: Policy Attitudes and Political Behavior in a Small Oregon Metropolis" (in mss.), June 1960. See also Robert E. Agger, Daniel Goldrich, and Bert E. Swanson, *The Rulers and the Ruled* (New York: John Wiley and Sons, 1964), especially Chap. 13, pp. 60 ff.

treatment is planned for the future, over half the respondents in the five poorer neighborhoods could not give any definition of urban renewal. In the six neighborhoods of somewhat higher social rank the percentage fell to about 30 per cent. Significantly, what they "knew" was almost entirely related to the improvement of housing.[5]

Such results agree with the estimates of officials in the LPAs:

"I'll bet you could ask the first guy you met on the street out there what he thinks about urban renewal and the chances are he wouldn't know the first thing about it!" [Small city, program twelve years old.]

"You talk to the average man about urban renewal and all he thinks about is 'tearing things down.' One guy thinks 'What'll I get paid?' and the other says 'You've got no right to take it from me.' Nobody ever heard of conservation, rehabilitation, and the rest." [Large city, program twelve years old.]

"Down in one Texas city where I worked there was an old Interurban Trolley being dismantled. Many people confused the two— thinking urban renewal was trolley removal. Most simply don't know." [Middle-sized city, program since 1949.]

This incompetence on the part of the public is certainly caused by both the complexity of the program and its novelty. Yet evidence indicates that neither the information policy of the LPAs nor the coverage given renewal by the press is calculated to develop an informed body of public opinion. Burd's study of the press coverage given the decision to locate an urban renewal project in a large Chicago area shows, in detail, how tardy, inaccurate, and inadequate was the information made available to the public. Kaplan describes the operational procedures of a successful renewal program:

[5]*Social Factor Analysis,* Research Department of the Health and Welfare Council, Inc., prepared for the Community Renewal Program of the City of Philadelphia, April 1964 (draft), pp. 78–85.

Outside of its attempt to stage the announcement of a project, however, NHA does not devote any substantial resources to publicity or public relations. Authority officials have said that too much publicity often stimulates organized interests that otherwise would have remained inert.[6]

Gans, in his treatment of the clearance of the Boston West End, shows convincingly the complete breakdown in communications between the Redevelopment Authority and the residents of the renewal area.

But Burd comes to the conclusion that the Chicago press is less "kept" than inept. It takes press releases from the Urban Renewal Agency and does not check their adequacy, while reporters in whose beat urban renewal falls depend upon agency personnel for their news (and value their sources). As Kaplan continues:

These dailies, like many other newspapers, define "news" as dramatic action or conflict. Since overt conflict among the renewal participants is infrequent, press treatment of local renewal is limited largely to formal announcements by NHA.[7]

The result is a lack of broadly based support for urban renewal, or even an understanding of the program.

The generalized uncertainty about the voter's understanding and support of the program is one basis for the Workable Program's requirement that there be "citizen participation." Such participation takes many forms. In a few cities there have been efforts to organize a broad network of citizen's associations for the program and to involve others already in being:

[6]For the Chicago press study, see Gene Burd, "The Role of the Chicago Daily Newspapers in the Selection of a Site for the Chicago Campus of the University of Illinois" (unpublished doctoral dissertation, Northwestern University Medill School of Journalism, 1964). The Kaplan quotation is from Harold Kaplan, *Urban Renewal Politics: Slum Clearance in Newark* (New York and London: Columbia University Press, 1963), pp. 32–33. Herbert J. Gans's report on Boston is found in *The Urban Villagers* (New York: The Free Press of Glencoe, 1962), Part IV.
[7]Kaplan, *Politics*, p. 33.

"The big fight created all kinds of forums for getting the thing out in the open. Business interests, who felt that if something wasn't done, Downtown would slip even further than it has, got involved. And then again, the importance of the program as an umbrella—political interests, business, labor, the Mayor, a lot of neighborhood organizations, all came under—and this is a city where neighborhood identity is still very strong."

Others however, rely chiefly upon the civic notables for their citizen's participation:

"I can look at an urban renewal program and see if it's going to go. If it goes well it'll have a commission that includes the power elite, or those who represent them. When I was in ———— I said 'Get yourself *top guys* on the Commission. Get rid of the oculist and the dentist and the other nice little guys who mean well and don't even get the complicated business straight in their heads—much less representing political opinion and power in this city.' "

Such efforts to coopt the civic notables may cost freedom of maneuver; on the other hand, the Citizen's Advisory Committee may be a victim of one way cooptation. An ex-member of one such committee put it this way:

"When I was appointed to the Citizen's Advisory Committee for Urban Renewal I didn't know what we were supposed to do. Then I found out that 90 per cent of the decisions were already made anyway and we met once a month to learn what other decisions they'd been making in the agency. Then it dawned on me that we were appointed to fulfill a legal requirement and that's all.

"When we did give them strong advice—to put that referendum off—they overrode us. And this was because the regional office put pressure on them, and *they* were under pressure from Washington to get something off the drawing boards and into the field."

When, however, urban renewal fails in a city through the operation of the political process, two diametrically opposite interpretations can be made. Some urge greater citizen involvement:

"Our mistake was secrecy. You need a widespread publicity campaign on something as new as all this."

And:

"We need national support, all-out advertising and demonstration. Now we can't use any federal funds in our locality, no municipal funds are available if anything's controversial, so we're left with *nothing* but citizen group support."

Others, however, take another tack:

"We've educated so damned many people I'm not sure we haven't defeated our purpose—they're all vocal. We use a Citizen's Advisory Committee, but I don't know if we should. Maybe the guys are smarter who play it cozy, with a few highly prominent people as window dressing, and do what they need to. I'm convinced you can't explain it to people—and I've worked like a dog trying to do it!"

And:

"Another crime was the cancellation of that S(————) contract because they didn't have a Citizen's Committee. We don't want one here—it would just be a divisive move, a way to organize your opposition."

So much for the citizens as voters who must pass on grants of money and power to the LPA. They are dangerous and unpredictable, because they would not like it if they understood it. Citizens are also involved, however, in code-enforcement, relocation, and the rehabilitation and conservation of neighborhoods. Experience with them in these efforts is crucial for the general success of the Workable Program. What has it been?

Code Enforcement

The existence of buildings that do not satisfy the housing codes is a result of either the recency of code adoption or lack of enforcement. It is assumed that for most substandard buildings the condition is a result of fiscal, not economic factors; that is, they are below code standards, not because of absolute economic impossibility, but because of a financial decision on the part of the owner. He has other things to do with his money. It is the task of the code enforcing agency to persuade or force the owner to bring the property up to code standards.

To do so is, frequently, to introduce new definitions that the owner has never heard of. Frequently he does not agree with them, and it is sometimes difficult to persuade him. A member of a Citizen's Study Group for Housing Codes remarked:

"Our opponents were asking questions about that code that we didn't have any answers to. And we still haven't found any to some.

"For instance, they've got a requirement that houses have hot and cold running water. I tried to look at it as if I were getting by on $3500 a year (or even less) and they required I have hot and cold running water. And I don't know, if they want to get by without hot running water and rustle around and heat their own, I think they have a right to. It doesn't hurt anybody else. Maybe if landlords who could give it to their tenants don't, it makes sense to require it. But for home owners I just want them to be clean, avoid contaminating the neighborhood—and that doesn't take hot running water."

The complaint about this provision of the standard and required codes was common; I found no LPA official who could or even *wanted* to defend it.

In one western city the housing code had actually been repealed, by initiative and referendum, endangering the federal certification of the entire local program.

Q: "Was your housing code, the one they repealed, enforced?"

Director: "Heck no. We didn't even try—those people weren't about to be made to conform. We did use it in our rehabilitation district, and that's where the opposition got its start—from some people who refused to let the inspector in their house."

"You would think the new subdivision districts, the ones that already comply and where the people are better off, would carry a vote for a housing code—for their own protection if nothing else. Only *one* did, out of a half dozen. Nobody wanted a housing code!"

In the West a number of persons spoke of a "regional" resistance to the program. "We're going very easy," one LPA director explained, "These people just aren't as docile as those back east."

But in a large midwestern city with a small proportion of substandard housing:

Q: "What do you do in the very bad sites?"

A: "Well, you do what you can. That's all. We have a category of secondary housing. We don't insist on separate bath and toilet facilities, for one thing. Other parts of the code make sense and are practical and we do insist on them, and we do limit the number of users of a given bath or toilet to eight individuals. This is something we *can* enforce, and the owners can bring it up to code."—Chief Housing Inspecting Official.

Although the regional explanation was current, it did not explain a situation that was relatively constant regardless of region. The codes were very selectively enforced. The most substandard areas were avoided, as were the best. At an extreme, the codes were applied only in the project areas, as in the quotation above, and at another extreme, the codes were systematically varied as they applied to different areas of the cities.

Another urban renewal official asked:

"What are standards for housing? Here in the west we're wasteful—
wooden construction, very cheap, very flexible, easy to rehabilitate.
Then we use them up, tear them down, burn them. That's very different from your cities of brick and masonry, huh?"

Both tactics were used in one large southern city:

"We use a different code for existing versus new building. In older
areas we take hardship into account, because when we enforce in the
rehabilitation area we are discriminating and putting a stigma on
the area.

Q: "How do you pick your (code) rehabilitation areas?

A: "Our logic is to try and hold blighted areas bordering on
slums."

And in another city the LPA official put it this way:

"Our code enforcement is the best I've seen. It's enforced throughout the city. We have a code adopted for this time and this place. It's
enforced the most consistently of any I've seen."

As we have noted, the logic of code enforcement assumes that it is
economically possible for all owners to bring their structures up to
the standard defined in the law. This is not the way those responsible
for enforcing codes see it.

"You'll never get code enforcement without two things first: (1)
You've got to change the laws so you don't capitalize illegally attained
values of the property condemned. Judges will listen to you on a
slum property, then they'll say, 'No-it's perfectly OK for the owner
to make big profits on an illegal shack'; (2) you have got to do something to subsidize the residents or owners that you find living in condemned properties. They have to have help."

Along the same lines:

"Our biggest problem with code enforcement, again and again, is the owner-occupied houses in old neighborhoods, inhabited by old couples. They *can't* afford to bring their house up to code—and they can't get a loan to do so if they could.

Q: "What do you do about them?

A: "You just do what you can."

In short, housing code enforcement is a new power of government in most American cities. It is not particularly popular with any large mass of the electorate and it is felt to work undue hardships on some property owners. These include people whose standards for housing are different from those of the American Public Health Association's Committee on Hygiene in Housing, as well as people who are economically unable to comply with the requirements of the housing code. Their room-crowding, windowlessness, plumbing shortages, and the like are not the results of preference but of lack of choice.

One code enforcement officer put it this way:

"No, there's a tendency for us to not let our right hand know what our left hand is doing. It's especially true with the federal government— those big agencies are so separated and specialized there seems to be a real communication problem.

"Take, for example, the National Security Administration. They give a widow on Social Security, at the most, $77 a month. Most of them have no other resources and that's supposed to pay for food, clothes, housing, medicine, everything. But we had an apartment house designed for us as an experiment, a real minimum job. . . . If it is paying taxes and interest on investment *it has got to rent for $75 a unit.* And these are units of only 336 square feet.

"So what are we saying? The widow either has to live on $2 a month after her rent is paid or she has to have substandard housing by those standards. There's real need for what we call secondary housing, and if we condemned it we'd wipe out the housing these people can afford.

"You see, the right hand is more likely to know what the left hand is doing down at the local level. It's hard to avoid."

Some Local Efforts

The net result of these problems is a very anemic program of housing inspection and code enforcement in most cities. Chicago has one of the larger urban renewal programs in the country; 2,798 acres are being "treated" at a cost of a fifth of a billion dollars of public funds.[8] Fourteen per cent of the city's 1,214,958 housing units were rated substandard in the census of 1960, a total of 169,664 units. And in 1961, 315,419 inspections were made by the Housing Bureau. That is, approximately one in four dwellings was visited by inspectors. Such inspections are usually in areas where the agency expects to find violations, yet only 19,373 notices of violation were sent, or about 6 per cent of inspected units. Though no data are available on violations voluntarily corrected, they must have been easy to secure for only 382 (or 391—data are confused) court cases were filed—one in every fifty cases of violation.[9] No wonder LPA officials in other parts of the country are skeptical. One spoke bitingly of

"The curious double standards the agency uses, raising hell over housing codes in Springfield, Oregon, while Chicago and Philadelphia go on as always. The blinders they use—while the situation is unchanged in those eastern cities because of corrupt inspectors and even corrupt magistrates."

[8] *Chicago Urban Renewal Progress Report* (Chicago: Department of City Planning, Third Quarter 1961), Table 6.
[9] *Program for Community Improvement, A Review of Progress*—1961 (Chicago: Department of City Planning, 1961), pp. 57, 75.

Nothing is known to the writer about any such corruption, but the data cited indicate the probability of discretion in the enforcement of the housing codes.

New Orleans is a city that has made a major effort to use code enforcement and private rehabilitation to raise housing standards. The city has no urban renewal program because of a crippling amendment to the Louisiana legislation. Nevertheless, it provides an indication of the limits and possibilities of code enforcement as a tool. In 1953, one-fourth of the dwelling units in the city were substandard, a total of 45,000 units. Over one-third of the population lived in them. The city invested approximately $100,000 a year in a systematic program of neighborhood inspection and enforcement and, by 1961, the Division of Housing Improvements had made 22,124 inspections and accounted for 16,862 abatements or improvements up to code. (It will be noted that the marksmanship of the New Orleans inspectors was better than that in Chicago.) The city officials used persuasion and tact; "hardship cases" were assisted to finance or to do for themselves, on staggered schedules, the necessary jobs. Only 5 per cent went to court.[10] At the end of nine years, approximately 38 per cent of the original substandard dwellings had been brought up to code.

Yet major questions must be asked. How many of the original occupants could afford to remain after the repairs? Millspaugh and Breckenfeld, in their study of the program, found that prices of rehabilitated dwelling space *doubled*.[11] The original renters often could not remain, and public housing in New Orleans has a waiting list of around 20,000. They are almost all Negro, as are the renters usually displaced by code-enforced rehabilitation. Such families could only have gone to comparable neighborhoods, finding homes among the 28,000 substandard units remaining. In the process, one would expect neighborhoods to be blighted as the demand for cheap housing

---

[10] *Reports,* 1953–1961, by the Division of Housing, Improvement of the City of New Orleans.

[11] Martin Millspaugh and Gurney Breckenfeld, *The Human Side of Urban Renewal,* ed. Miles L. Colean (New York: Ives Washburn, Inc., 1960), Chap. III.

increased, however mean its quality. As for the Division of Housing Improvements policy for these neighborhoods, some local housing experts were queried:

Q: "How good a job is the Division doing?
A: "It's doing a splendid job [laughs]. But only a job in the easy areas.
Q: "What happens if they inspect the hard ones?
A: "There'd be a big political backfire.
Q: "Do you think it could be forced through?
A: "I doubt it."

Asked what would happen to the "rock bottom slums," another official answered:

"The Planning Commission uses the theory that the private market will take care of it, but they've been there now for twenty-five or thirty years and nothing has happened. We've made a study of slum owners. They bought at depression prices and they've made profits many times over their original investments. If they sell they have a big capital gains tax to pay."

Meanwhile, the private housing market in New Orleans is chiefly producing new-tract housing for middle-class whites in Jefferson Parish and in "New Orleans East," a lakeside development within the city limits.

In short, the process of code enforcement creates severe strains upon the city agencies responsible. They modify these strains through (1) selective enforcement by areas within the city, and (2) the use of different standards for different kinds of people, neighborhoods, and housing. There is evidence that much housing can be brought up to code standards with a sufficient investment of time, attention, and skill. But this is possible only in certain kinds of neighborhoods and with certain kinds of people. For others, code-enforced rehabilitation means economic bankruptcy, eviction, and either a net loss of housing (if the house is owner-occupied) or a movement to a new and different substandard house by the renter. Threats of such action may produce a backfire in the urban wards. As one code enforcement officer put it,

"When a council passes a housing code they are setting up *the legal definition of humanly habitable housing.* Most legislative bodies don't know what they're doing when they do it. They think it's some sort of statement of minima, or aspirations. Then they find they've made it the law of the land.

"Of course the question won't arise if you just pay lip-service to the housing code, as most cities do."

Rehabilitation and Conservation

The programs for the rehabilitation or conservation of existing neighborhoods require widespread support from the residents. They must be prepared to invest in their own houses if they are substandard and they must even face the possibility that their home will be condemned and razed, making way for the homes of others with higher incomes, or for nonresidential uses. The LPA needs their cooperation because a loss of confidence in the neighborhood can lead to a rapid increase in blight, as maintenance is dropped and illegal uses multiply.

The LPA is required to invest heavily, in scarce manpower and in ingenuity, if a neighborhood is to be mobilized for such a major collective undertaking. The LPA is also, frequently, faced with serious handicaps. One that is increasingly important is its own past: The first projects put into operation have typically been "clearance and redevelopment." These have resulted in a net loss of low-cost housing—the kind important to the residents of rehabilitation areas. After this start, the LPA must make clear to the residents the difference between redevelopment and rehabilitation.

In one city whose urban renewal program was stopped dead as a result of political opposition, an earlier redevelopment program had razed thousands of houses, overwhelmingly occupied by Negroes. As a Negro spokesman remarked, "Urban renewal ran into trouble in the inequality between the compensation given and the prices for other homes anywhere. When people sold they couldn't buy again, given our land prices and house values." Since the area was in the center of a local politician's strength, "He sent out postcards to everyone showing how they'd lose their homes and have no place to buy a new one." As an observer remarked, "They were shacks to the Housing Authority, but home and security to the people. They went from home ownership to tenancy."

In another city a redevelopment program had destroyed a neighborhood which was a thriving ethnic community. The LPA officials (not the ones responsible for the program) were asked if various accounts of the operation were accurate.

"It's essentially true, but it wasn't our responsibility. We have to say, 'How do you live with this and overcome it?' I'd say we wish there'd never been such a project. I don't think anyone realized the degree to which that thing embittered all kinds of people. You can say that you won't do it again, but until you've done enough to prove it they won't believe you. We've done everything to allay these fears. We have expert assistance, a master relocation plan. But it's slow work."

LPA officials have become very skeptical of the earlier, unassisted types of rehabilitation. There is little support now for "do it yourself" projects based on the 1954 amendments to the Housing Act.

"We had one project, what they called unassisted—they got no public help except a little better break with the mortgage, not enough to make up for anything. There was an awful lot of resentment over it."

Another official spoke in similar vein of a similar project:

"Nationally we're making a lot of hoopla about conservation—nobody's doing it, of course. But we can't talk about rehabilitating these eighty-year-old stucco-and-wood frame houses. Even if you could do it physically, the pressures of population growth and economics are such that you can't give thirty years of economic life to the damned places.

"If you'd seen what was done in ——— with that 'rehab' project. It's a close-in downtown slum. To rehabilitate and assume they'll look like they do now in thirty years—it's ridiculous! You should see some of the borderline cases. They'd make you cry. People who invested $3,000 in houses to bring them up to code on the basis that you're building for long term stability. It's just not fair!"

Another of the difficulties in rehabilitation stems from a simple matter, but a basic one—time. The time-lag between the designation of an area as a rehabilitation area, final approval by the administration, and work in the area, may be very long indeed. Yet the need to protect the integrity of the program requires the safeguards, in the form of URA rules, which spend out the months and years.

"The Neighborhood Rehabilitation Program won't work. It's awful. You have to designate areas beforehand, long before, and when you do you stir up a neighborhood for years. Nobody wants to put in any improvements on a house that's going to be destroyed.

"You see, your program goes so slowly, because of the agency rules and the problems of organization, that you take a long time. And that very loss of time changes your possibility of ever doing anything like your original goal. In fact, with a slow program, Urban Renewal is a blighting program. It is *responsible* for blight."

The "halo" effect of previous redevelopment projects, the enormous time lapse, and the great investment of LPA time and energy in coping with local communities and political pressures, have led some to dismiss the rehabilitation program as unusable. David Wallace comments on the Philadelphia program:

Completed in 1956, the CURA study took a pretty objective look at Philadelphia's realizable renewal goals over the next 18 years. Not a program really to deal with obsolete structures, mind you, just the substandard ones. . . . With this relatively modest program, annual net expenditures were to be at the rate of $45 million a year, twice the previous level.

Today, only a small part of this program is still proposed. Conservation didn't really get launched before it was further reduced in favor of Penn, Drexel and Temple [i.e., three local universities that were given the lion's share of Philadelphia federal and local moneys]. In one major area where it was tried it ran head-on into politics. This is a clear example of what I mean about the unpopularity of urban renewal as we now know it, once it is really understood by politicians and their constituents. I strongly suspect that the city was very relieved to get off the hook when the institutions "blackmailed" it into diverting the funds allocated to conservation.[12]

And in Newark, where an agency devoted to rehabilitation as renewal policy had decided on an "unassisted" program for ideological reasons, the social processes simply moved too fast.

But the rapid progress of Negro invasion, over-crowding, and illegal conversions in that area eventually challenged NCNCR's initial assumptions about the efficacy of private renewal action. . . . Throughout the summer of 1957 the amount of public construction and the extent of spot clearance planned for Clinton Hill steadily increased. In August, with estimated capital expenditures in Clinton Hill well over a million dollars, NCNCR voted to apply to URA for a fully assisted program.[13]

Nevertheless, scores of general neighborhood rehabilitation projects are being planned around the country. Forty-three have been completed to date, 87 are under preparation. And the city of Boston projects eight in its ten redevelopment areas.[14] Nor does the program appear hopeless to all responsible LPA officials:

"When they've seen what it is, they can understand. For instance, we've had many people around the project begin to rehabilitate for themselves. And we've had local people near the project call us, and

12Wallace, "Beggars," p. 49.
13Kaplan, *Politics,* p. 88.
14*Report of Urban Renewal Operations* (Washington D.C.: Urban Renewal Administration, December 1961), Table ii; *The 90 Million Dollar Development Program for Boston* (Boston: reprint, *City Record* issue of September 24, 1960).

ask when they were going to come in. But they have to see it and see that it's doing good to understand it or support it."

Officials in the Housing Authority of the city of Little Rock are among those who are enthusiastic about rehabilitation. Their "Livestock Show Area Project" is one of the most often cited examples of effective rehabilitation. In an area including 296 families, 168 brought their houses up to code standards, and 75 new houses were built or are in process of being built on lots cleared of the hopelessly deteriorated structures. One hundred twenty-eight households had to leave the area, but of these, 122 were rehoused in standard housing within their means, and only nine households were placed in public housing.[15]

Such an achievement requires, however, a supply of standard housing that the displaced households can afford. In Little Rock such housing was available at prices ranging upward from $30 per month. In many cities, matters are otherwise. In Chicago, for example, ". . .the mean gross monthly rent paid by households with incomes of less than $2,000 is $61."[16] This is for all housing, standard and substandard. Furthermore, most of this housing is not accessible to Negroes. The results are clear: "Urban renewal means Negro removal." Rossi and Dentler document the wide differences in housing standards between Chicago whites and nonwhites in their study of the Hyde Park-Kenwood projects. In summary:

> The community was viewed by Negroes as an almost ideal residential location, far from blighted or deteriorated. For Negroes from every class level the unrenewed community was so much better than the "ghetto" from which they had moved that the importance ascribed by whites to renewal

---

[15] *Relocation in the Livestock Show Area of Little Rock, Arkansas,* A Report (Little Rock, Arkansas: Housing Authority of the City of Little Rock, May 1960), Tables 1 and 2. In another project where urban renewal was used to expand a Negro college campus (Philander Smith College), no dwelling units replaced those destroyed. Yet the percentage living in substandard dwellings dropped from 56 per cent to 19 per cent with relocation.

[16] Beverly Duncan and Philip M. Hauser, *Housing a Metropolis—Chicago* (Glencoe: The Free Press, 1960), p. 143.

seemed only a flimsy excuse. Except at the uppermost level of the Negro community, renewal plans were seen as directed specifically against Negroes.[17]

Despite such problems, Chicago continues with its programs of conservation and rehabilitation. Yet political observers voice concern at the long-run consequences. Rehabilitation can be defined as a program to "get the Negro out" by the large Negro electorate for whom good housing is a rare commodity. It can also be defined as a program that is dispersing Negroes through new neighborhoods, tipping *them* toward all-Negro occupancy, by the whites who fear Negro "invasion."[18]

The "white backlash" has been documented for Newark. Kaplan shows how the relocation from a central Negro neighborhood speeded the invasion of nearby Clinton Hill (incidentally destroying chances for a rehabilitation program) and notes that many white informants see the Housing Authority "as an agency that 'takes care of the Negroes' and helps their dispersion into white neighborhoods."[19]

Relocation

No aspect of the urban renewal program has excited more concern, polemics, and political anxiety than the problem of relocating those whose homes are destroyed. Humanly, the matter excites concern; it is "pushing people around," and generally the poorest people with the fewest choices. Theoretically, it is argued that if urban renewal shifts people from one substandard house to another, it is merely slum-shifting; if it is bringing about a net loss in low-cost housing, it is in-

[17]Peter H. Rossi and Robert Dentler, *The Politics of Urban Renewal* (New York: The Free Press of Glencoe, 1961), p. 38.

[18] See, for example, discussions of the motive power behind rehabilitation in the "Back of the Yards" district. Most observers conclude that it was aimed at keeping the Negroes out. Millspaugh and Breckenfeld, *Human Side.*

[19] Kaplan, *Politics,* p. 156.

creasing the slums by putting pressure on a wide array of deteriorating neighborhoods.

The national program has, over-all, cleared property which is 85 per cent residential; redevelopment plans indicate new uses will be only 50 per cent residential. Even in the Little Rock project discussed above, there was a net loss of 53 dwelling units, nearly one-fifth of those originally in the neighborhood. And in the Philander Smith project, whatever its value, 89 units were destroyed—39 of them "standard" housing.

The national program has resulted in the destruction of four dwelling units for each unit built. This is, to be sure, based on projects in being and not projects completed. But even when only the latter are considered, the cost is two destroyed for one built—and these completed projects probably reflect disproportionately the earlier program that allowed only 10 per cent nonresidential. The new housing built usually cannot be available to the population that lived there before. It must rent at higher prices. Thus old inhabitants are unable to return to the redeveloped or upgraded areas.[20]

The logic of the Workable Program demands that there be enough housing of standard quality and comparable prices within the city to house the displaced. It does not, however, spell out the ways and means of getting them into it, beyond the government-granted moving allowance, with a limit of $300 per household, and this is no protection against a second move. Yet, for the program to work perfectly, all who could afford standard private housing would move to it and all others would move into publicly subsidized housing.

Unfortunately, many of those displaced cannot even afford public

[20] For the four-to-one figure, see Martin Anderson, "The Federal Urban Renewal Program: A Financial and Economic Analysis" (doctoral dissertation: Massachusetts Institute of Technology, School of Industrial Management, 1962). For the figure on completed projects, see Jerome Rothenberg, "Economic Evaluation of Urban Renewal: Conceptual Foundation of Benefit-Cost Analysis" (preliminary draft of report to the Brookings Institution). Rothenberg's data are based on URA files. The data for the Little Rock program, highly esteemed for its concern with the housing goal, led to similar conclusions; four structures are destroyed for each one built (and some of those built are nonresidential). "Information Sheet," Housing Authority of the city of Little Rock, April 20, 1964.

housing. In one city the lowest public housing rental was $40 per month; furthermore, those mothers drawing Aid for Dependent Children and having children under five could not qualify, nor could those with "morals records," jail time, poor maintenance habits, and the like, nor those persons under sixty-two and without children. The destroyed area had included many units renting for $18–$20 per month; it was a slum area, with a slum economy. Secondhand stores, cheap eating places, more or less illegal amenities, as well as economic opportunity in the form of trash and bottle salvage, had made it a viable location for some of its residents. Since public housing was out of the question for them, many people moved to housing renting for well under $40 per month—sometimes as a result of new conversions. Of 144 cases handled by this LPA relocation service, only 13 per cent ended up in standard housing.

When it is well within his means, standard housing is still not necessarily attractive to the displacee. The LPA cannot force him into such housing while substandard housing, condoned by the enforcement agencies, exists and is available. This led one LPA official to conclude:

"It's *extremely* important that an effort be made to inform and sell people on places they ought to move into that are decent, safe, and sanitary. You just have to live with them. It's not enough to hand them a pamphlet—somebody's got to give them a selling job. It may take two days, but what the hell are we trying to accomplish if it's not to help people. It's in relocation I think we've failed most miserably."

The relocated person must be persuaded that the dwelling unit is worth the price, compared to his other consumer demands.

The Relocation Staff was surprised to find a number of younger couples in the area content, or seemingly so, with their present circumstances. In most cases both husband and wife had jobs and were in a position to improve their standard of living.

> Five "shotgun" shacks jammed together and facing the side of a corner lot presented the worst example of substandard housing in the Livestock Show Area.
>
> These five rental shacks had no running water or natural gas. One structure had electricity; the families living in the other four used kerosene for heating and light. Three outdoor privies and a single water faucet served all five families.
>
> Living in the middle one of the five shacks—and thus the closest to the water faucet—were a school teacher and his wife. He was also a preacher and part-time barber. She worked in a clothing plant. They paid $10 a month for their home.[21]

In such cases, the relocation officers simply have to create "the revolution of rising expectations." And the *Relocation Report* notes that, in the opinion of the author, "they also paid in lost social status that was essential to the man's profession as a teacher." And—"The five shacks were the first acquired and demolished by the Housing Authority. The school teacher was comparatively sophisticated and depended very little on the Relocation Staff for finding a new home. Provided with an FHA Section 220 loan, he built a new house in Granite Heights, a private subdivision. . . ."[22]

Even when the displacees recognize the value of standard housing and can afford it, many resist a movement away from a familiar community.

"When we relocate Negroes, we're accused of ghettoizing them—though they came from all-Negro neighborhoods to begin with. We did search, and we found areas of good housing where Negroes were accepted. But the minute we went south of the River, where Negroes have never lived, they began to get nervous. They didn't want to be pioneers—leaving their neighbors and community. It's easy enough to understand."

The irony of requiring integrated neighborhoods for displaced Negroes is thus compounded: Negroes relocated from urban renewal

---

[21]*Relocation in the Livestock Show Area*, pp. unnumbered.
[22]*Ibid.*

project sites are usually the poorest and least educated—exactly the opposite of those most interested in living in integrated neighborhoods. (Though there are very few instances where housing open to Negroes is located in the outer areas of the central city, officials in three such cities spoke of the reluctance of Negroes to move so far from their community.) Some would think it unfair to make the weakest and most poorly motivated carry the burden of radical social change.

In the general opinion of the public and the professional renewer, the substandard housing area is simply a trap. For the ethnic enclave, it is viewed as a ghetto and some redevelopers have the feeling that scattering the ghetto is in itself a good thing. However, dozens of studies by sociologists indicate that the ethnic enclave is as much a *protective community* as it is a restrictive pale. And, when a protective community is destroyed, the personal loss of the displacees is another major cost of relocation. In a dramatic article, Marc Fried has reported on the reaction of the Boston West Enders to the destruction of their neighborhoods. Seventy per cent of the sample had considered the West End to be their real home; of these, over two-thirds manifested symptoms of severe grief and loss at its destruction. Fried concludes:

> Grieving for a lost home is evidently a widespread and serious social phenomenon following in the wake of urban dislocation. It is likely to increase social and psychological "pathology" in a limited number of instances and it is also likely to create new opportunities for some and to increase the rate of social mobility for others. For the greatest number, dislocation is unlikely to have either effect but does lead to intense personal suffering despite moderately successful adaptation to the total situation of relocation.[23]

West Enders lived in their area through choice—nearly half could have moved if they had wanted to and only 14 per cent had planned to leave before relocation forced them out. To be sure they did not

---

[23]Leonard J. Duhl, ed., *The Environment of the Metropolis* (New York: Basic Books, 1963), includes both the Fried article, "Grieving for a Lost Home" and an article by Edward J. Ryan, "Individual Identity in an Urban Slum," documenting the importance of *choice* in the location of people in the West End.

always foresee exactly what the cost of leaving would be. Gans quotes some informants:

> Most people were not very explicit at that time about their feelings toward the area. Since the West End still existed, and since they had never known anything else, they could not estimate how its disappearance might affect them. "What's so good about the West End? We're used to it," was one quite typical comment. Subsequently, however, I heard more anguished remarks that indicated how important the area and its people were to the speaker. In December, 1957, the day after the federal government gave the city the go-ahead, one young Italian man said: "I wish the world would end tonight . . . I wish they'd tear the whole damned town down, damn scab town . . . I'm going to be lost without the West End. Where the hell can I go?" [24]

Relocation may be such a thorny problem that an LPA tries to avoid residential areas entirely.

Q: "How is it that you've escaped the community criticism you ran into in _____?

A: "We left the residential areas alone, and where we did relocate —near the south end of town—the people are groups that don't matter [i.e., skid roaders, Negroes]."

Or concentrate, as the above makes clear, on areas where the relocatees will not have too much political "clout."

"A lot of the opposition on that project was, you know, the little old lady in tennis shoes—opposing for good and sufficient reasons—a loud and vocal opponent. But that kind of organization is possible for only a short while, then it dissolves.

Q: 'Has there been a response from ethnic minorities?

A: 'So far it's been minimal, because our projects are highly con-

---

[24] Gans, *Urban Villagers*, p. 289.

centrated with the Spanish-speaking, and they aren't too organized or vocal.' "

Another tactic is to supply housing near the project. This is congruent with a frequent finding: Relocatees tend to return to their same general neighborhood.

"The residential area is fairly highly integrated today. We may be able to make modestly priced housing available nearby—across the [main thoroughfare], for instance, is a neighborhood that's been under study for years. There's been a lot of pressure—*affirmative pressure*—for rehabilitation action there from the residents, and they're mostly Negro."

In general, if adequate housing is available and financially within the means of the displacee, there still remains a complex and demanding job of persuasion for the LPA. As the relocation officer for a local agency noted for its "clean" relocation work put it:

"I was in charge of relocation and my assistant was a colored woman. She's now supervisor of relocation. We had the same office, desk to desk. It helped show people we weren't using urban renewal for Negro removal.

"You've got to help people understand renewal. I know that when you first start out with surveys, you can tell people a lot that'll help even if you can't give them exact detail. You can tell them what it's all about. You can tell them you're their friend—You think it's silly to tell a guy, 'We're going to take your property,' and he's still my friend? We don't.

"We say, 'To do this project right we're hoping we can buy your property.' (Of course we *can* take it.) Then we can show him his alternatives—and he'll come along. I discovered this for myself. We were having some trouble, things were slow. I said, 'Let me take over some cases.' I finally took the hard cases, the ones who refused to sell. I ended up with only one court case—and that was a twenty-foot piece of vacant land. He went to court and finally got almost exactly what we'd offered in negotiation."

Such patience and expertise are not universal in relocation offices. In one project, in which many thousands of residents were displaced, only *one* social worker was employed. Relocation was a matter of waiting while they scattered. Such "relocation strategy" is comparable to the bookkeeping methods which equate "relocation" with "displacement" and report them together to the URA.

Relocation is, in some cases, heavily dependent upon public housing as an alternative to the destroyed stock. Here also the score varies greatly—by the existence of housing alternatives and by the persuasive ability of the relocation officials. In Little Rock the proportion of the displaced who end up in public housing runs under 10 per cent, but in one northern city it is very much higher.

Q: "What will you do about those others, the ones with less than $4,000 per year?

A: "My experience indicates we will take care of 50-60 per cent of 'those others,' in public housing. The rest don't want public housing— or rather, there are two types of them, those who dislike public housing, feeling they'd be regimented and spied on—and those who can't get in at all because their situation is so absolutely hopeless. . . .

Q: "How many accept it, who're qualified?

A: "From the _____ project we had 1800 families, two-thirds Negroes. About 60 per cent of the eligible Negroes went into public housing. One reason is simply the tight restrictions on Negro housing [here]. We used the public housing people as the relocation agency; they did a wonderful job. There was a lot of hand-holding between Housing Authority people and the relocatees. When the relocatees see what they can get in public housing, versus what is available on the private market, they're sold."

Public housing will hardly solve the problems of those who dislike it. In one city, where only 20 per cent of the relocatees went into public housing and the rest chiefly into substandard housing, an LPA official said:

"Relocation is the biggest mess *in urban renewal,* not just here in _____. We've got a lot of things we have to do we haven't been doing. First, we've got to put more emphasis on the sociological factors. Second, we've got to have a closer tie-in with social agencies. Because we need much more work on picking up those families—you've got to get control and knowledge of the families during the planning process. Long before execution you've got to answer questions of the sophisticates. You've got to get backed up with background information and you've got to account for before and after on all your families. You've got to know."

But in another region of the country, where relocation has not been an issue in public controversy, an official held the opposite opinion:

"The record isn't bad. Seven per cent end up in substandard housing, 10 per cent get lost. But what of it? Is it a real world we're living in? We've got to work with the communities as they are, work on *building* relocation housing. Take a progressive city of 100,000 with 28 per cent substandard housing: If you relocate people, wouldn't it be strange if they all went into the standard housing? *We need more housing.*"

It is indeed a real world the various LPAs are living in. Some are under fire from Negroes who are a quarter of their city's electorate; some are under fire for "scattering" them; some are under fire from civic leaders who detect a callous treatment of the poor; some are under fire from economists and curbstone sociologists who see their programs as "relocation of slums"; as a result, all are subjected to an increasingly close scrutiny by the Urban Renewal Administration.

Relocation requires that the displaced persons cooperate closely with the agency that is displacing them. It requires that they rely on the agency for help in relocation, accept the agency's definition of suitable housing, and then afford it financially. It also requires that somebody provide "decent, safe, and sanitary housing" for those whose incomes are below $3,000 a year, and below $2,000, and below $1,000—those on social security, old age pension, or nothing at all. They must accept public housing if they qualify: If they do not qualify they must get by with substandard housing—or with no housing at all.

Chapter 4

THE LPA AND STATE AND LOCAL GOVERNMENT

The LPA typically has powers only for land clearance and re-development and limited powers for the rehabilitation or conservation of existing neighborhoods. Thus for the Workable Program to work, a wide variety of other governmental agencies must somehow be induced to cooperate. The state government, through its existing property laws and enabling legislation, sets the basic charter within which the federal program is feasible. Furthermore, through such massive action as the state-guided Federal Highway Program, key decisions on the city's future development are made at the state level. Then various local agencies are important; code enforcement is typically assigned to a bureau of the city government; public housing is a separate bureaucracy again, in fact if not in name. Local capital improvements are the result of ponderous and complex administrative machinery and local referenda. All must be coordinated if the program is to be effective.

The State and Urban Renewal

All but three states have passed enabling laws for urban renewal. However, consent may be given grudgingly and may be withdrawn.

The Florida Supreme Court has ruled urban renewal unconstitutional under present law.

"Now the federal government won't go on until we get either a court decision on our [local] act or a state act. There's a move for this. We even got to committee.

Q: "Why do you have trouble in Tallahassee?

A: "You've got two states, north and south. Those crackers up there, they say 'Urban renewal is nothing but public housing and you know what *that* is—those guys in Washington say there ain't no more niggers!' But the Florida legislature is generally conservative. If you bring together the feds, housing, and Negroes, then you've had it.

Q: "But how about public housing?

A: "That battle's died down. We have 4,000 units here, all de-segregated. You see, public housing originated during the depression and a different socioeconomic situation. And they're already established. If they hadn't adopted one then, and you tried now, you'd get nowhere."

Resistance in Louisiana is somewhat more complex. There is the usual blame placed upon the "rednecks" from the country.

"We have a big problem—urban renewal is at least ten years away. It's the big city against the rest of the state. To try to get the stigma away from the city, legislation was introduced by Lafayette, a little town upstate, but they saw through it in Baton Rouge."

But others point out that the battle began in a New Orleans ward. Said one sociologist:

"Urban renewal was killed by local New Orleans politicians. You see, the area to be redeveloped was the center of strength for Comiskey, Morrison's major opponent. Comiskey and his supporters upstate backed an amendment which restricted condemnation for Urban Renewal purposes.

"Now there is pressure from upstate cities—and downtown New Orleans businessmen, because the latter are losing their trade."

The politically dynamic nature of the issue is clear in this situation. Ideologies of racial segregation or states' rights confront those of downtown renovation and slum clearance. Politicians whose strength is in the slums resist fiercely the erosion of their support, joining with upstaters who are against Negroes, cities, and the "feds."

At the opposite extreme, some states have programs that completely bypass the local electorate and give great freedom to the LPA. An LPA official in one western state expressed his satisfaction in the situation.

"No, there are no provisions at all for referenda. There's been activity in the legislature lately to add requirements, but the state law pretty clearly intends to give urban renewal freedom from the objections of everybody owning land in an area—otherwise they'd all object (it's their nature)—and you could never get anything done."

However, in this state there are indications of opposition brewing in the legislature. Another official:

"You get it alright—down south. But that's idiot country anyway—there's no crazy idea in my time that didn't arise there. There's also stirring in the smaller cities—ethnic minorities are objecting to redevelopment in their neighborhoods. We'd have run into a lot more trouble in this town if I hadn't taken steps to draw the fangs on it.

"You see, it's a political matter. The worst time I had in the legislature was with the politicians whose intuition told 'em there was a groundswell of protest back in their districts."

Hazarding a guess as to the roots of opposition in this state, one official remarked:

"You get a conflict with values when land is being redistributed. That has many social ramifications. Fundamental here is the nature and growth of the community—this town has always been, basically, a real estate promotion. There's a widespread retention of the traditional real estate philosophy here.

Q: "Is it the real estate groups who oppose you?

A: "Not any more—at least there's been a national change of policy in the Real Estate Board. But the notion of a public agency taking land is still a bitter pill to take."

In general, the LPA officials in this state were sanguine about their support in the legislature, and this, in turn, shielded them from the public response of the citizens. On the other hand, a political grass-fire similar to the one lit in the New Orleans wards could endanger their freedom and power.

Much more general is the problem of the federal highway program, a large part of which is now focused upon cities. It is administered through the state highway departments and, although the building of the freeway network in a city has crucial effects upon land use, there is no device which forces coordination of urban renewal and highway planning. One can see some consequences in the short run:

"Another thing about the [urban renewal] program for central Negro areas. The highway department has just located a cloverleaf right in the middle of it. It was done carefully—like the story of Epaminondas (you remember?)—he was careful like his mother said. He put his foot exactly in the middle of that pie. Well, that's how the interchange sits in the urban renewal area."

In another city urban renewal was stymied for months because of uncertainty as to the location of a freeway and its access ramps. "It affected the use and value of our entire parcel. When they changed their mind, we had to develop a complete new set of studies of marketability and the like. We couldn't affect *them,* and we couldn't go on without their decision. The State Highway Board wouldn't decide—and so we couldn't even begin to sell property!" When asked about his own relations with the City Planning Commission, he said, "We try to go through them—though we have full powers to do anything we want."

The highway program affects urban renewal in another way. It displaces thousands of persons and, since the land is frequently chosen because it is cheap, it cuts through the same kind of neighborhoods as urban renewal. Yet there has been no relocation program for these displacees, and they compete with the urban renewal displacees for new homes. Regarding the cloverleaf in the "central Negro areas" one informant said:

"The highway program has *no* provision for relocation. I forced them to set up an agency, collaborate with the city government and send people into the area to calm people down, talk with ministers and organizations. How many are affected? I don't know; they estimated 2,500 under the old plan, and it'll be many more now."

The long-run consequences of the highway program are crucial for urban renewal if areas within the city are to be revitalized for new uses. For the use and value of space in the city is largely determined by possibilities of movement. However, no LPA observed had been able to integrate its long-range plans for the city with those of engineers in the state department of highways. One official was asked about the consequence for his program of transport study findings that indicate nothing but dispersion for the residential population of his metropolitan area:

Q: "How do your assumptions jibe with those of the [transport study]?
A: "We're going with them on our own CBD projections, but in

residence we expect central-city development as well as suburban development.

Q: "Do you think they overestimate the suburban development?"

A: "No—not if population growth continues. They'll be OK. For example [in one central city residential area] we'll put 8,000 families there—maybe 30,000 people. But what's that? A drop in the bucket for the city as a whole—and for the metropolitan area, it's really nothing."

Thus the urban renewal program in this particular city is based on the assumption that downtown residences will be in increasing demand, while the local transport officials are assuming the demand will drop compared to that for suburban areas.

One official was discussing cooperation among local authorities. He was asked, "What of the highway department? Do they cooperate?"

"We have a coordinating committee—which is not a good coordination device. When you get to it, you find the highway is already planned. But communication helps—you at least have a chance to get your assumptions in order. But we *still* have the highway departments putting the cloverleaf in the middle of the project area."

In short, the urban renewal agencies are informed after the decision and are then able to adjust their program (or "assumptions") to whatever the highway department has decided. This, in turn, is usually based on a simple extrapolation of past trends in traffic demand, modified by economy and efficiency—the straightest line through the cheapest land.

The LPA in the Municipal Government

Although municipal government is of importance in highway location decisions, and can be politically important at the state level, it is crucial for four functions in the Workable Program. In relocation, as we have noted, public housing is basic in some cities; code enforcement is theoretically basic in all; municipal capital improvements and land-use planning are obviously major determinants of a program's effect. Each task is usually allocated to some separate bureaucracy.

In some cities the LPA *is* the housing authority. In such cities, evidence suggests the relocation function is carried out more carefully and effectively.[1] This may be through the use of public housing for displacees but in Little Rock, it will be recalled, less than 10 per cent chose public housing. A more important reason for the correlation of effective relocation with public housing authorities as LPAs is probably the fund of knowledge and the experienced personnel in the Housing Authority *who are committed to housing.*

In general, LPAs want to maintain a clear organizational distance between themselves and public housing. Public housing is not popular today.

"The first project was solely in the hands of the Public Housing Commission. The realty board, apartment house associations, home builders, all saw it as just an excuse for more public housing. The defeat came about because there was strong feeling against the Housing Authority, plus their way of proceeding, which was criticized.

"They had a large staff, they operated rather freely, and some felt they had unlimited dollars and staff. The City Council decided to put it up to a vote of the people. [What?] A bond issue for the local cash contribution. It was defeated in a fairly close vote.

"Public housing is unpopular and a lot of people link it with urban renewal."

And:

"The Housing Authority here is the LPA. This is due to the political strength of the program, and it's a reasonable choice, though maybe not a good one.

[1] Duggar, "Federal Concept". See also his paper, "Politics and Administration of Urban Renewal," presented at the meetings, American Political Science Association, September 1960.

Q: "Why?

A: "They went at their task in a way similar to that of the public housing program, using a pretty high-handed approach. The selection of sites and what you do with them was determined by decisions in a well-knit and politically cohesive group.

"The Public Housing Authority has always had an extremely bad reputation, one that's been unfortunate nationally because we have a big program that has had a real impact on the city. It's results are now one of the major problems of the city.

"I regret this because I started out in public housing and I still think it can and needs to be done."

While public housing may be accepted in many cities, it is not liked. It is a necessary evil. When urban renewal was separated from public housing, the possibility of expanding the program in Arkansas improved at once.

"Since we got that state law changed [allowing URA outside the Housing Authority], we've got urban renewal in Blytheville, Fort Smith, Pine Bluff, other places. They didn't want anything to do with public housing, but with urban renewal they've all come in."

And in another region:

"When we pulled away from the Housing Authority, suddenly we were nice guys!"

The separation of the LPA and the public housing program is politically expedient, but it has many consequences for the program. At an operational level, it may weaken the effectiveness of relocation generally and use of public housing in particular. (In cities with waiting lists of 20,000 for their public housing units, whether or not displacees from project areas are given precedence may be an administrative decision in the Housing Authority.) The separation may also prevent the use of persons with long experience in rehousing the poor and a knowledge of procedures that have been found effective.

But beyond this, the separation of urban renewal from public housing weakens the program's emphasis upon "eliminating and preventing slums," for the latter requires improvement of housing. (To be sure, such a change in program objectives may be exactly what is desired. One LPA official stated bluntly: "I think urban renewal should be taken completely out of the housing program.")

Code Enforcement.   This task is usually not handled by the LPA itself. It is delegated to an agency of inspection. It is another unpopular function and undoubtedly the LPA officials are glad to have it performed by others. (As one remarked, "It's a problem, but it's not *our* problem!") Code enforcement may elicit agreement in the abstract; in the concrete it is unpopular:

"We lose the intent sometimes. We come to the city and the intent is to upgrade a given area. You are supposed to upgrade and prevent spread of blight. Now the administration of HHFA could come into [here] and see that all this hassel is about a housing code that nobody ever did anything about anyway.

"What could be done instead? Use a code for 'rehab' only, to show people what could be done with it. Sell it. Start then with some pissy little code that didn't mean much, and gradually make it more complete."

Whatever the virtues of this suggestion, it is not operating procedure. The Workable Program requires a code that, literally interpreted, means a great deal. And it is not popular with those who must enforce it.

"We have double standards for building—black and white—and a convention of corrupting the building code. The housing inspector subcontracts to the building inspection department. But they like new buildings and hate old ones—hate to have to inspect them. And they won't enforce the code. The director of the housing department doesn't like the job because he's basically a planner. It won't get done."

Code inspection can and does get done, however, in the specific areas chosen for urban renewal projects. Chicago has an urban renewal task force that inspects for all kinds of substandard conditions at the same time, as does Baltimore and other cities. The logic is to do the job in stages: In practice, enforcement is generally limited to target areas selected because (a) they are "easy" or, (b) they are urban renewal project areas. The program rarely gets beyond these stages. Yet from a highly respected LPA official:

"I've said for years urban renewal and public housing won't get rid of slums. Only way is through enforcing codes, taxing, and financing. This is where the importance of enforcement comes into play. Of the seven points of the Workable Program it deserves the greatest emphasis.

"There are a limited number of cities with enforcement programs. You can name them on the fingers of a hand. I told the Mayor seven years ago we had to do it, it was absolutely necessary. He agreed, but then he didn't and complained about the difficulty of getting personnel for the department. I told him, 'Some day you're gonna get caught—people are going to burn up in these damned fire traps.' Sure enough, it's happened."

The LPA has neither the power nor the "line" responsibility for code enforcement. Everything depends upon the political leaders, who may or (more usually) may not see the organic relation between overall code enforcement and their urban renewal program.

Capital Improvements.   The building of streets, schools, parks, playgrounds, and parking facilities are all important for urban renewal. They are, first, substitutable for cash in the local contribution to a project's cost. And, secondly, they are integral parts of over-all plans —to rehabilitate neighborhoods, to redevelop areas. Yet such capital improvements can be problematic for, whether they are forthcoming at all, and where they will be located when they do, are subject to the local political process.

Many observers remarked on the immediate effect public improvements can have upon areas to be rehabilitated. "The building of streets has the most startling effect," a member of one city planning commission pointed out, "once the street is in, with curbs, you begin to get concern for yards, rehabilitation of structures, upgrading in general." But in the fiscal conditions of many municipalities, streets and sidewalks, curbs and drainage are luxuries. "There's a crying need for public improvements to go in, when they bring their structures up to standard. People expect it, and then we can't come through."

Such improvements rest upon the city's ability to tax or to finance through bond issues. And these may very well be at the mercy of the voters:

"The people had voted $8,000,000 for a new auditorium. They were also thinking of a new campus for the college. Urban renewal was seen as a tool for accomplishing clearance and site preparation for both, which would be close together, with a parking facility to be used in the daytime by the college, at night for the auditorium.

"Then an east-side car salesman created a diversion. He got an initiative in to prevent it from going on the west side. 'Eighty per cent of the people live on the east side,' he said, and so on and so on—and finally killed it. The site was sensible and fit in with the plan."

Now the college and the auditorium are several miles apart, and the parking facility is unbuilt.

But in general the large capital improvements which are part of the community's contribution to the project cost are relatively easy to coordinate with the other work. Difficulties occur when such powerful and autonomous forces as the Federal Highway Program are involved, or when the timing of supplementary local investment in rehabilitation areas is in issue. Beyond these lies the more general problem: How shall the over-all capital improvement program be related to the over-all planning of the city? The formal agency supposedly responsible for these matters is the local planning commission.

The Local Planning Commission

Local planning bodies are common, if not universal, among cities participating in urban renewal. Their function, however, is almost always *advisory* to the central political body; at most, they can delay action a month or so. Frequently they are either not consulted or they function as a rubber stamp of approval. Projects are thus lent a seal of purity with very little meaning. In his study of urban renewal in Newark, Harold Kaplan underscores the impuissance of the city planning office.

> The city planners arrived late as a claimant on the local renewal scene, having neither the inclination nor the staff to assert the values of central planning before 1956 or 1957. By this time, however, the basic configuration of NHA's [Newark Housing Authority's] settlements had been established. The planners had the choice of either "playing the game" in the hope of some marginal gains or attacking "the system" from an external position of outrage and impotence. Finding little support at City Hall or among the "civic leaders" for their attempt to bring NHA within the ambit of a master plan, the planners soon lowered their sights and made their peace with Danzig [the LPA director]. In exchange for their guarantee of routine approval for all future NHA sites, the planners accepted Danzig's promise that "central planning considerations" would be kept before NHA's staff in planning future projects. Danzig further promised that the City Planning Officers would be fully informed and consulted on all NHA activities in the Central Ward.[2]

One reason for the weakness is the lack of theoretical rigor in most "city plans." So broad and loose are these maps of the future that any one of a nearly infinite set of projects may be acceptable. Such projects can be designated in a very short time:

[2] Harold Kaplan, "Urban Renewal in Newark: The Power Structure of a Successful Program" (paper delivered at the 1961 annual meeting of the American Political Science Association) p. 9.

". . . an odd thing happened here—understandable, but I sometimes think it's been a curse. Back in 1951 when we felt we should take advantage of the new federal laws, the Planning Commission right off the bat designated fifteen very large areas scattered through the city as redevelopment areas.

"When the question: Where shall we start? came up, the physical thing was determinate. [That place] was an interesting feature, covered with deteriorating buildings, on a site overlooking the city.

Q: "It was esthetics and centrality of location?

A: "I think that about summarizes it."

Planning bodies do not have any basis for priorities. So grandiose are their dreams that they see "need" broadcast throughout a city. (The city referred to above, for example, has among the lowest proportion of substandard dwellings in the nation.) The open-ended definition of blight means that "anything goes."

As one consequence, there is little real resistance by planners to what is designated as "blighted." Sometimes the potential market value of an area is such that it is marked for clearance and redevelopment when most structures are sound and rehabilitation would be in order. Gans defines the West End in these terms; 40 per cent of the dwelling units were in good condition, 34 per cent fair, and the remainder poor or worse. As he points out, other areas in Boston were much more deteriorated. But "planning" turns out, too often, to consist of speculative judgments about the future salability of the *cleared* land.

In Newark, the Planning Board "defined its role as that of a judicial tribune, which would make no independent investigation of its own. It would hear evidence presented by both NHA and the opposition and then would reach a decision on the existence of blight."

Despite the claim of judicial impartiality, it soon became apparent that most Board members were already committed to finding blight in the North Ward. In the weeks immediately preceding the hearing (the Planning

Board) agreed that the blight hearing should be simply an opportunity for the opposition to air its grievances. CPB members discussed with NHA officials how to prevent site residents from disrupting the hearing and discrediting the project.

It is no wonder that, later, one planner remarked that "Every few weeks . . . we open the newspaper and get hit with another clearance proposal for ten, twenty, or thirty blocks." These are often areas diagnosed as appropriate for rehabilitation by the Planning Board.[3]

The impuissance of the planning commissions in city after city allows the urban renewal authorities a free hand in determining "blight." As Kaplan bluntly remarks, the Newark Housing Authority viewed "central planning as unrealizable, utopian ideal."[4] In truth, the lack of a defensible set of priorities, together with their political weakness, has meant that planning commissions are generally bypassed in decision. Theoretically crucial, they are actually of marginal importance to most urban renewal enterprises. Though LPA officials may have a pious regard for "the planning commission," and try to "go through them" in reaching their decisions, most have the power to do about what they like.

The LPA and the Metropolitan Area

Planning is crippled in any event by the limited political jurisdiction to which any plan may apply. Today an urban housing market, transportation system, and labor force are metropolitan in scope, for men may move long distances across the contemporary urban complex. But urban renewal is limited to a given municipality. However

[3] For the discussion of Boston see Gans, *Urban Villagers,* pp. 314–318; Kaplan discusses the Newark Planning Board in *Urban Renewal Politics,* pp. 118–129. Quotations are from those pages.

[4] Kaplan, *ibid.,* p. 116.

massive the programs, they operate only in the central cities, and this circumstance drastically affects a program aimed at either eliminating slums or rebuilding the city.

Code enforcement can only be expected, at most, in the municipality presenting the Workable Program. Yet across the invisible boundary lines there may be no housing code at all and little in the way of building codes. The proprietors of rooming-houses and tenements in such jurisdictions can set up stiff competition for the conforming proprietors in the renewing city, and this may be taken into account by the building inspector of the latter. More important for many urban areas is the development of substandard housing out in the "boondocks," the unincorporated rural-urban fringe. A large proportion of our substandard housing is located there, and it is being built there today.

"Do you know what we need to do with urban renewal in this part of the country? Not downtown reconstruction, but the fringe areas. So we could clean up the fringes and then annex them to the central city. And when we talk about a workable program, it's impossible on the fringe. You can't adopt a housing code for a county; fifty per cent of this one is federal timber. But the fringes are not in any city.

"We recently annexed this big fringe area. It's like most of them in this part of the country—they're all decayed. If you used a housing code for these places there wouldn't be any housing left because they're *all* substandard."

One is apt to forget that a very large part of the substandard housing in the United States has not deteriorated; it was built to low standards and it is still being built.

Governmental boundaries also affect slum elimination when they serve to fragment the housing market. As slums are destroyed the ex-slum dwellers are supposed to move into better housing, vacated in turn by those who have improved their lot. But when municipal boundary lines are used to keep out Negroes and other ethnic minorities, the supply of housing available for them is severely restricted. Relocation and "trickling down" of houses are both usually confined to the older center of the metropolitan area, a restriction that encourages use-crowding, segregation, and the transplanted ethnic slum.

Even if the aim of a program is "to rebuild cities" rather than to eliminate and prevent slums, it is still hamstrung by governmental fractionation. While new land is cleared at great public cost in the center of the older city, construction hurries apace in the pastures and fields of the fringe. Penn Center, in Philadelphia, is impressive as an effort to bring the dead to life; the rapid development of industry and housing at Valley Forge is impressive as a new scene for life. The plans for downtown all rest upon the belief that the location is valuable, but suburban advantages continue to lure investments that give life to an area. As this results in new residential suburbs, industrial parks, and shopping centers, the CBD engages in a tug-of-war with suburbia. The sharp conflict of interest is manifest, for instance, when transportation planning and land use are at issue.

To be sure, metropolitan government is not a serious problem to the officials in the LPAs. They are, after all, arms of the central city government. They accept the boundaries and the limited jurisdiction and work within them. In the process, however, their own program may suffer greatly—they may hasten the deterioration of the CBD by overbuilding for a limited demand; they may hasten the decline of neighborhoods by eliminating Negro housing already in short supply in their city; they may acquiesce to transport developments that hasten the movement of the middle-class Nordic white Protestants to suburbia.

This does not bother them materially. After all, there is no organized group to speak for the interest of the metropolitan "community." As one official put it:

"[A professor] asked me what we needed in the way of metropolitan integration of our program. I said [grins], 'Friend—we don't need *any* integration with those buggers. We've got enough problems of our own and we're doing OK without tackling the whole damned metropolitan area!' "

The LPA and the Real Estate Industry

When a local program condemns land for clearance, it must have assurance that the land can be resold for acceptable uses. The same is true of "spot clearance" in rehabilitated areas. When an owner is forced to improve to code standards there is a presumption that the market value of the rehabilitated property should bear some relationship to the increased investment. All of these contingencies point to the basic importance of the real estate market.

In redevelopment, particularly, the land cleared must be desirable and the terms of sale must be feasible. Land that is now occupied by slums would not necessarily be useful if cleared: "People are not standing in line for slum property." The result is a tremendous pressure to designate only land which will be marketable when cleared.

Q: "How do you choose a site for a project?

A: "Economic feasibility, plus whether it's a beneficial project. You can't take 'blight' and just go around the city. If you study your problems . . . find where existing blight and economic feasibility coalesce, then you can move. Then you'd have the necessity of proving it to a lot of people.

Q: "But what of the areas where you just have blight?

A: "I wouldn't touch them."

The result of these pressures has been the designation of close-in blighted residential neighborhoods, to be redeveloped as commercial and institutional sites with a net loss of housing (if any housing at all is built). It is by no means certain that this can be done forever.

"I don't think urban renewal will continue indefinitely just limited to CBD development. I think, in fact, that will slow down. You know, there's only so much land a central business district can use—beyond that point you'll just give a city economic indigestion."

In the meantime, however, economic feasibility has rigidly dichotomized areas. And even when areas are possible "100 per cent corners," money has not been necessarily forthcoming.

"The real difficulty is that each developer proceeds on the assumption that he'll put the fewest nickels of his own money into the job. Now they don't usually put much of their own money into any project.

"One guy bidding for a project running around $75,000,000 had the gall to brag that he was putting $35,000 of his *own* money into it! Of course, he was an ass and he didn't get the job, but that's an example.

"In renewal work a private developer has to be ready to spend six to eight years on a project. It takes time and it takes patience. Most of them don't have either the time or the money to do it."

It is indeed a difficult and a time-consuming process. The Philadelphia urban renewal program is one of the best staffed, best supported, and most effective in the country. Yet their estimated "normal" time for a project is five years, while the variation in time consumed at each step is as great as from one to thirty-five months. (And there are six steps in planning and approval *before* execution.) Kaplan's data on the Newark program are in general agreement; of sixteen projects announced between 1952 and 1959, four were completed by 1960. The average time from announcement to "open for occupancy" was just under six years, and two of these projects were entirely made up of public housing. For the redeveloper, it is a long and costly process which freezes his movement over a period of years; for this reason it is not attractive to some firms and it is impossible for others.[5]

The dependence of the program on the private developers allows the latter a counterpressure on the program. This increases in strength as the size and complexity of the project limits the field to a few very large firms specializing in redevelopment work. The selection of sites and the nature of redevelopment may both be affected. Kaplan speaks in these terms of the Newark program:

> Slum clearance policy in Newark can best be characterized as the product of adjustments in the goals of NHA's professional staff to meet the demands of private redevelopers and of the federal housing agencies. The detailed plans for most of the nine projects were agreed upon in private negotiations between Danzig, private redevelopers, and federal officials, and then quickly ratified by local officials as an integrated, unamendable "project package." [6]

In Kaplan's opinion:

> They were determined not to begin another project without first having secured a redeveloper and tailoring the project to his needs. "We took an awful chance in the North Ward," one official said, "by guessing at what redevelopers wanted. Then we had to go around peddling vacant land. Now we let the redevelopers *tell* us where they want to build." . . . The new rule was: "Find a redeveloper first, and then see what interests him." [7]

---

[5] For the data on Philadelphia, see *The Redevelopment Authority Program, 1945–1962*, Technical Report #6 City of Philadelphia: (Community Renewal Program, September 1963), p. 85; for Newark data, see Kaplan, *Urban Renewal Politics*, pp. 8–9. For a general discussion of the problems from the redeveloper's point of view, see Eli Goldston, Allan Oakley Hunter, and Guido A. Rothrauff, Jr., "Urban Redevelopment—The Viewpoint of Counsel for a Private Redeveloper", in *Law and Contemporary Problems*, Vol. 26, No. 1 (Winter 1961), pp. 118–177. As they note, "Counsel for the prospective private redeveloper will soon find that an urban redevelopment project is 'just another real estate deal' in the same limited sense that Alfonso's first evening with Lucrezia Borgia was 'just another blind date'" (p. 119). They emphasize the evolving creation of both a legal system and ways of operating it in this novel area.

[6] Kaplan, "Urban Renewal in Newark," p. 2.

[7] Kaplan, *Urban Renewal Politics*, p. 24.

In theory, competitive bidding is the ideal mechanism for disposing of land. Both the price and the design may enter into the competition. In fact, the great majority of redevelopment contracts has been handled through private negotiation, as in the Newark case.[8] It is easy to see why. With respect to a large project, attractively sited, one LPA official said:

"Only community services can be negotiated now. We've just finalized our competitive bidding system. If the market won't make it work we can use minimum appraisal and negotiate sales.

"Very few people are interested in taking the chance you must on a competitive bid. They can't plan. Then too, we've had some sad experiences—the Golden Gateway was negotiated at too low a price and they had to ask for more money."

Another official:

"We've had some successes and some miserable failures. It's not a perfect mechanism because after the competition the market comes into play. It sometimes turns out that the basis on which you sold the land has to be changed—then people say you've got to reopen the original bid. You could even have lawsuits from unsuccessful bidders."

This same official went on to discuss the conflicts within the agency between those concerned with market values and those concerned with other values.

"Are we just trying to sell real estate? Or are we trying to rebuild our cities? I have this battle right here in my own office. I hear a real estate disposition guy argue, 'We're in the real estate business.'

[8] As of 1960, 78 per cent of the transactions reported by HHFA were disposed of through negotiated sale. See Lyman Brownfield, "The Disposition Problem in Urban Renewal," *Law and Contemporary Problems,* Vol. 25, No. 4 (Autumn 1960), p. 749.

But I have to watch it, too—there's GAO [Government Accounting Office] and they'll say we didn't get enough money for the land.

"I'd like to explore ways in which we can make disposition more effective. Our regulations treat this as a market operation, a real estate program. It's not. We're surrounded by red tape making it very hard to do what I'm interested in—which is to rebuild cities."

The negotiation of sales results from relative lack of demand for the land. Attractive alternatives are available, while building under redevelopment rules is a long and complex process. Thus lack of competitive demand leads to the dominance of a few large redevelopment corporations and to negotiated sales. The LPA, willy-nilly, must adjust to the real estate market.

"There are about six hundred cities in this program now, and it stands to reason a lot of them are worrying if they can sell that land. Look at Detroit. But it's not a question of the economic feasibility. It's a question of time, patience. These cities are in the real estate business and they might as well realize it and tackle it from that angle."

Thus the LPA is under pressure (1) to choose the most marketable sites, in order to retain leverage over cost and future uses; and (2) to adjust to the requirements of the large redevelopers when the sites are not exceptionally desirable.

"That project . . . was never developed because of the rugged terrain and poor planning—multiple ownership. We're putting up a community of 8,000 homes there. You don't have to do your work in the CBD; this project will return a lot of juice. Our third project is one that was old slum; it will be a high-rise, urban neighborhood. We're going to create an urban, midtown neighborhood for people of middle income.

Q: "Couldn't [the first project] have been redeveloped by the private market?

A: "Oh, of course they knew it would be extremely lucrative. In fact, people have tried to develop it before, but they couldn't get control of the parcels. Here's where the right of eminent domain is important in urban renewal.

Q: "Any problem with land disposition?

A: "We get such prices we cry on our way to the bank. We *would* like to get a broader array of income classes in urban renewal projects, but we only have a few places for households with under $8,000 a year income."

The resulting dilemma, from the point of view of a planner and architect concerned only with "rebuilding the city," is made clear in a recent statement by Minoru Yamasaki, an architect and designer who has worked on redevelopment projects.

"I think it is marvellous that you've tried various ways of getting good designs. But—is it possible to limit those who build buildings to more idealistic people? . . . The federal government is giving out great prizes to these people—that is, it's easy for them to make good financial gains—and for that reason it should be possible to make sure that those people live up to their responsibility for this privilege." [9]

This concern was common among those LPA officials who defined their job as one of "rebuilding cities."

"I'd insist on substantially higher standards for building design, too. Until recently—maybe, because of the traditional separation of church and state, the state can't be godly—we've had lousy design. Now we know we've got to take the programs and public funds, take hold and be exciting, stir the aspiration of the urban citizen. He's capable of electing people who'll spend his taxes wisely and, at the same time, make a beautiful city."

[9] Speech at National Association of Housing and Redevelopment Officials Workshop, Eugene, Oregon, July 8, 1962.

Economical Limits and Cultural Limits

Although the hard economic limits are inescapable in redevelopment, cultural limits seem equally rigid. The real estate industry has, as Grigsby notes, paid little attention to innovation in *marketing*.

> . . . the brokerage industry is business antiquity in its supinest hour. Absorbed with the task of professionalizing their group, brokers have failed completely to consider the possibility of influencing aggregate family movement, and thus their own incomes, by new and imaginative sales techniques.[10]

The demand for housing and other facilities is simply extrapolated from the past, with little concern for broadening the market. The Urban Renewal Administration has remarked upon the blindness of the construction industry to the lucrative market possible through rehabilitation and conservation; it has even published a pamphlet demonstrating what can be done.[11] And Yamasaki posited, as one explanation for the dreary nature of redevelopment design, "the commissions going to older, more irresponsible firms with—you know —political influence."

The sheer economic limits of what can be done with the private real estate industry by LPAs, based upon what will profit the former, cannot be known with certainty until innovation is more normal than at present. Here urban renewal, as a radical effort to achieve new goals, highlights the rigidities of the existing system. Committed to the private market in building, the LPAs cannot afford to allow that market to operate without controls: All possible goals would be sabotaged in such a gambit.

"You can't use the market, and the market alone, for determining land use. Because of the money market you get the greatest possible

---

[10] *Housing Markets and Public Policy,* p. 212.
[11] *Home Improvement: Lessons From Experience,* Bulletin 2, Urban Renewal Service.

capital available for *service stations*—rather than for more desirable uses."

Still the horns of the dilemma are close together. Land acquisition continues to outrun disposition—and disposition is far ahead of completion. As Mayor Peterson of Minneapolis put it:

> When the site acquisition and clearance have been completed, there still remains the problem of site disposition to be followed by rebuilding. It is this stage of the urban renewal program which we are anticipating with excitement. Until we reach this stage, what we are accomplishing is destruction. What we destroy we plan to replace with something much better, but I believe Minneapolis will be best served if we do not carry forward a program for tearing down part of our city faster than we can execute the companion program of rebuilding.[12]

And an LPA Director spoke ruefully of a project which had gone "sour."

"Our project turned out to have undersoil water. We sold all the land but we haven't got one building started. The people who own it are in a quandary. We aren't responsible and we sold it in good faith, but for two years nothing has happened. And it looks bad."

Caught between the inexorable chain set in motion when land is acquired, on the one hand, and their plans to eliminate slums and rebuild the city on the other, LPA officials walk a narrow line. As one put it, "We struggle, negotiate, compromise." But they need the new construction, the propaganda of the deed; in the process of achieving it, they accommodate to the market, interpreted by the demand of the private real estate industry. This is, of course, the mechanism that produced the original "problems" to which their program is addressed.

[12] Quoted in Brownfield, *Problems,* p. 732n.

Chapter 5

THE SHAPE OF THE PROGRAM: LOCAL PROJECTS AND FEDERAL CONTROL

To get the money and buy the sites, the LPA must have support from the local and federal governments. The documents must be signed and money guaranteed locally; the URA must accept documents and disburse federal funds. Beyond this, the voters and their representatives, other relevant agencies, and the private market, all together, constitute the relevant organizational environment in the locale. The amount of pressure that these bodies can put on the LPA depends upon the seriousness with which the LPA is committed to the broader aims of the program and the rigor with which the URA enforces its demands. When men work in such a complex situation, their efforts are first oriented toward stabilizing fronts. That is, some of the necessary forces are guaranteed through a working agreement with whoever controls them, reducing those that remain problematic to manageable dimensions. What tactics are used by the LPAs?

The voters are stabilized by one of two methods. First, and very popular with those who can afford it, is the program completely shielded from the voters. This requires that local officials concur, that moneys be available without referenda, and that the initiative be avoided. Securing the funds may be managed in several ways; through the regular tax revenues, through special district bonds, and through capital investment counted as a local contribution in the project site. (As one LPA director remarked, "Thank God for the School Commission; they're rich. And if it weren't for them we'd be out of business.") If one is so unfortunate as to work in a state where the initiative and referendum are legal and popular, the best strategy is to develop a statewide law and program, making referenda complex and expensive propositions for the opponents.

If, however, the local voters must be called upon to vote for the program or its financing, then the strength of the existing political control apparatus must be mobilized for urban renewal. Under these circumstances, the LPA must work for popularity and nothing works like the support of a popular mayor. The bonds are usually included in a long list of other bond proposals, meant to support such items as highways and schools. Since the citizens do not understand urban renewal, the avoidance of referenda or the packaging of urban renewal with conventional issues of local politics, may be used to *insulate the program* from the voters. For, if a governmental program is exposed to the opinions of the voters, it cannot go far above their modal level of commitment and competence without failure. Given voter distrust, it must then either be backed by those whom the voters trust, or be insulated from the voters altogether. A party machine and a popular mayor can combine the two strategies. In sum, the more directly democratic a local urban renewal program is, the more likely it is to live from hand-to-mouth. Since, however, powerful organizations must be able to predict if they are to make great investments for long periods of time, order is created, even if this requires undemocratic means. The alternative is interorganizational anarchy, chaos within the program.

As for the other crucial governmental agencies in the city, they are each accommodated in a fashion. The responsibility for code enforcement is delegated to an existing department of city government, and few questions are asked. The Public Housing Authority becomes a standby agency, legally acceptable as an outlet for the relocation requirement of the Workable Program. The City Planning Commission is consulted when appropriate (that is, after the basic decisions have been made). The private real estate industry is consulted before decisions are made, and the "political settlement" derives from what it will do and what the LPA sees as the best bargain possible between the demands of local leadership, on one hand, and the federal agency on the other.

Decisions on projects are usually based on shaky empirical findings, sometimes on mere beliefs. What is the demand for standard housing among slum dwellers? What is the demand for CBD cleared lands for all purposes? What will be the net effects of the project in terms of Program goals? Marketability studies are rarely adequate to the load they must carry, for they ignore the competition of sites scattered throughout the metropolitan area, are carried out long before the land can be offered for sale, and hardly ever incorporate the final aims of urban renewal as variables. When empirical knowledge is unavailable, the usual decision is based upon law, ideology, rules-of-thumb—in short, an extrapolation of what has gone before within the limits of political expedience and administrative rules.

This chapter shows how some of the local movements for urban renewal got moving and how the project sites were chosen.

The Local Projects

Many projects seem to be chosen for show. That is, they are "unsightly" places that people see. As George Duggar put it, "Place after place I visited, particularly in the South, when I asked them 'Why did you pick this particular place?' they would say 'Why that's the place that everybody sees.' " [1] Projects are usually in the downtown section, in areas bordering high-rent neighborhoods, or, as in Savanna, places the tourists see when they come into town.

And what are these places like?

[1]Personal communication, January 9, 1962.

"Public interest in urban renewal really goes back to . . . *slums.* Respected people in the community look at slums and say, 'It's a problem.' Then if you can get dedicated men to work with them and show them what can be accomplished with urban renewal as a tool —you can begin to solve those problems."

The problems are, significantly, *problems of the respectable people,* the urban middle class. They are not problems of the slum dwellers. They are sometimes the problems seen by those who have a stake in the central business district.

> *Q:* "Why is your program only CBD in orientation?
> *A:* "The groups that backed it were interested in the downtown."

Their interest may center on areas which are far from being slums in the view of outsiders, as well as that of the people who live there. Gans has documented the discrepancy between most definitions of slums and the areas chosen for redevelopment in Boston: ". . . the majority of the structures provide low-rent rather than slum dwellings. . . . Nor does the West End satisfy the social criteria which would make it a slum. There are 'problem residents' . . . But these problems are not created by the neighborhood." In Gans' opinion,

> The certification of the West End for redevelopment was not due solely to its physical and social characteristics. Because of its central location adjacent to Beacon Hill and near the downtown retail area, real estate men had long felt the West End was "ripe for higher uses." [2]

Across the country in another large city a similar area was chosen for the first urban renewal program. In the words of the local LPA director:

[2]Herbert J. Gans, "The Human Implications of Current Redevelopment and Relocation Planning," *Journal of the American Institute of Planners,* Vol. XXV, No. 1 (February 1959), pp. 17–18.

"The project was proposed early in 1952. A group of interested people formed a large citizen's committee, and they suggested this and two others. They made some very superficial studies and alighted on it as the most logical place.

Q: "Why?

A: "It was an area with considerable substandard housing [many third-generation families] which could readily be converted to an industrial park and should be, given the city's zoning and the facilities in existence, and the plan left room to get materials into factories. Then there was serious conflict of land use. Industrial blight hurt the residential areas, and *vice versa,* they prevented expansion. But it was still *heavily* single-family dwelling unit residential.

Q: "Who pushed it?

A: "The head of the Industrial Committee of the Chamber of Commerce and some Housing Authority people who cared about getting rid of substandard housing."

In another city the thrust for urban renewal was due to the local newspaper crusade, "Progress or Decay." It was supported by three successive mayors from both parties. The area chosen was, according to the LPA director, "for display purposes. It was in the city center, near the depot—obviously terrible slums." Another project in the same city was justified in these terms: "First, it was ringing the downtown, and second, it was a stretch of endless crappy housing. There was no place to cut it off—it was all bad." In one city which had just designated a renewal area, the director was asked: "How did you choose the area for redevelopment?"

A: "First, it's the largest area we have in the central city. Second, it's the site of the expressway interchange. Then too, it's an obvious slum area. Also it's in the center of the city, which is very cooperative.

Q: "What about marketability?

A: "We've done no studies yet—we'll do a general study. The area is too large for one project, and relocation(which is going to be a big problem) is too much for one project.

Q: "What will the future use be?

A: "It'll have to be higher density—the land is too valuable.

[*A Colleague*]: High density residential is the best use.

Q: Residential for whom?

A: "*If* these people moved back, $65–80 is the highest they could go. I don't know if that can work in this area."

The prime movers are not necessarily oriented toward personal profit. There is frequently something that one can only call civic patriotism uniting the group pressing for urban renewal. It blends nicely with financial interests and the dependence of the program on the real estate industry forces such a blend of interests.

"Many people here are committed to the city, and were interested in getting off the ground and stimulating the economy. Then later we had the formation of a [citizen's group]. Urban renewal has been well supported. Since we passed the state law, *no* dissenting vote has been cast in either the legislature or the City Council.

Q: "Why does it appeal?

A: "Well, first there's a real emotional appeal—the conservation area [an area of old mansions near the CBD] means a lot to people, and we're going to conserve it under section 220 rehab. Then there are dollars and cents interests—the transport center development, which will help downtown."

And sometimes the movers are political leaders who see a chance to unite a following.

"There was inactivity on the program for years, then an upset election. _____ came in as mayor, a dark horse who got the rebellion vote. He knew it wasn't for him, but was against _____ . He felt there was nothing for him to lose, politically, so he decided to put himself behind a few good programs, to create a 'new look.' He's

quite a remarkable man. Some of his close supporters were urban renewal fans and they have the inside track of those who were 'loyal
before '32.' Urban renewal is used as an umbrella kind of activity.

"Oh yes, there are some major liabilities in the program. But
when a man comes in as a dark horse with no personal loyalties, he
has to find something big enough and bold enough to make him into
a positive choice. For him there isn't any good alternative. It's something of a gamble, and maybe it doesn't pay off.

"It is recognized that there must be the delivery of enough products by the time he comes up for election so that he'll have something to speak for. It is also recognized that he is the man who is
responsible for the program's getting as far as it has."

The programs are, then, pushed by people who have very particular interests—in the downtown, in political success, in sites for apartment houses. Nor do most programs, as they accumulate over time,
have any particular logic. An unusually perceptive official described
his program this way:

"You see, the program was really started expedientially. For instance,
enforcing the smoke control ordinance forced _____ to a decision,
because they had a giant plant on the other side of the river that was
in violation. But they wanted to expand their plant and comply with
the ordinance. But they couldn't get the land because of holdouts. So
we went to bat and got a huge investment of new plant, right in the
city limits! The tax base alone was worth it.

"Then _____ said they'd build downtown if we'd guarantee occupancy—and we went out and got occupancy committed for twenty
years! This building you're in right now was once _____ ; they told
us, 'We'll move downtown if you'll sell our building.' We bought it
from them.

"The _____ project started with a million-dollar donation for a
civic auditorium, to house the opera. It was not only a good location
for the auditorium, it was also a logical target for renewal.

"So all our projects were expedient decisions. Then we had three university neighborhoods, near the campus, all blighted, which we made available for campus extension."

Most of the projects described in the latter quotation were privately (locally) financed. Many LPAs, however, are under pressure to get some of the free federal money. "Tell the people their dollars are being used all over the country to redevelop cities—and especially in Puerto Rico, where they're spending billions on a bunch of lazy baboons!" [sic].

So marked has been the concentration of support among commercial interests and those committed to downtown that some officials are frankly cynical. Though they discuss the Workable Program with approbation, they do not see it as a significant target in their city.

"This program is basically an economic program—it's not a program against blight. Sure, some social workers and planners want to make it into that. But most cities don't give a damn for blight.

"Why do you get concern for the central city at all, the CBD? The real surge nowadays is for the removal of CBD blight. Why? Here they can see real economic interests at stake. As for housing—there hasn't been a social will or social machinery to get the residential blight job going."

Or, as a knowledgeable director put it:

"This is not a welfare program—it's economic self-interest. They know if they're going to keep making a buck something has to be done about the decaying parts of the city. On the slum program, we've got an intensive program getting industry interested in hiring Negroes, combining it with a neighborhood rehabilitation program. It's obvious. These unemployables are going to stay around and they're going to cost us all money if we don't do something about them. The welfare program grows right out of economic self-interest."

In short, the programs arise as a response to what are defined, locally, as "problem areas" in the cities. Civic entrepreneurs, newspapers, business leaders, and political officials spark the efforts. Programs are sold as economically beneficial to the city (meaning the commercial interests) and, particularly, those with a stake in the CBD. Projects are chosen in an expediential fashion from those areas that (1) look bad to the groups mentioned above, and (2) can be profitably redeveloped. Nor should this be surprising: The feasibility of the program depends upon economic demand in the private real estate market and, aside from the civic leaders and downtown interests, no other segments of urban society have any great interest in urban renewal.

Federal Control

If urban renewal is to be anything more than a gigantic public works program, if it is to be addressed to eliminating and preventing slums and blighted areas, the URA must insist upon the terms of the Workable Program. This is a formidable assignment; the LPAs are integral parts of the local political process and, as a result, tend to temper the wind to the local lambs. Evasion of the rules in code enforcement and relocation, planning, and citizen participation, is commonplace among the local agencies responsible. The LPA, in balancing its precarious load of commitments, tends to vary its emphasis among aspects of the Workable Program in the interest of getting on with the job, of "getting something off the drawing boards."

The URA, in turn, varies its emphasis in different parts of the country and among the wide array of cities participating. There is pressure on the national office to show results, thus the pressure upon the various regional offices. The results show up in discretionary decisions where particular local programs are concerned. Kaplan has said of the URA in the 1950's:

> Embarrassed by the number of vacant sites throughout the nation and anxious to justify their requests for larger urban renewal appropriations,

URA officials have maintained a steady stream of federal aid to Newark. As long as Danzig could produce redevelopers, URA was prepared to wink at his violations of the Workable Program.[3]

George Duggar puts it in more charitable terms:

> Since the central government wishes to get on with the job of renewing the cities it tends to use the project and workable program procedures as minimal protections for the central government's expenditures. . . . the workable program (sic), in particular, is administered with flexibility, the central government demanding somewhat more each year from each city, but not necessarily the same performance from all.[4]

The federal system and the "joint cooptation" which is its result produce a chain of interdependence. The LPA must depend on the City Council, the Bureau of Building Inspection, the Public Housing Authority, and other organized groups, yet it cannot control them by fiat. The URA, in turn, depends upon the LPAs: It *can* control by fiat, but its chief weapon, suspension of program funds, hurts the URA in its self-defined purpose. As a result, the URA is in local politics, in the hundreds of cities with projects.

From the point of view of the LPA official the insistence upon the Workable Program requirements frequently seems just one more problem in a maze of problems. "What we do is too little, too slow. The process is like a can of worms. It's an extremely complicated legal and financial and mechanical process." And many LPA officials, facing the political consequence of URA's insistence on the Workable Program, are bitterly critical of it.

John Lange summarizes the results of a questionnaire study of LPAs, in which they were asked about the "most difficult" elements of the Workable Program.[5] The rank order of difficulty, with the number of cities choosing each element, is as follows:

---

[3] Kaplan, "Urban Renewal in Newark," p. 3.
[4] Duggar, "The Federal Concept in Urban Renewal," pp. 44–45.
[5] Quoted in Duggar, "Politics and Administration of Urban Renewal," p. 20.

		Number	Per cent
1.	Relocation	70	43
2.	Financial Ability	53	33
3.	Code Enforcement	45	28
4.	Citizen Par'n	40	24
5.	Comprehensive Plan	13	8
6.	Administrative Org'n	10	6
7.	Neighborhood Analysis	7	4

(The total number of cities was 163; per cent does not total 100
   as some named more than one element as a problem.)

The table must be read with the foregoing discussion in mind for,
if the URA is not insistent, an item is no serious problem. Even with
the past leniency of URA demands, however, major portions of the
Workable Program are among the most difficult aspects of life for the
LPA. It is clear that the "most difficult" elements are those that require the kind of cooperation the LPA has no formal power to demand, where compliance depends upon the insistence of local political
leaders or the cooperation of community leaders and citizens. Con-
trariwise, the "least difficult" elements are those solvable through
administrative fiat. A comprehensive plan may be planned by planners; administrative reshuffling is a favorite game of administrators;
neighborhood analysis can be delegated to hired staff. Not so with
relocation, financial support, code enforcement, and citizen
participation.

In general terms, LPA officials object to the contents of the program, the rigidity of the program, and the personnel of the regional
offices. Their criticism of the planners is particularly bitter.

"They're going to have to eliminate planners wanting to be administrators. Planning is an element, but it's not administration and it
can't be.

Q: "What kind of planning efforts do you object to?

A: "Well, planners look at it all from a beautification point of view

—not what the community can and will afford, but what the planner wants.

"And then—each project has different problems, and planners often don't recognize these differences. For example, our project is a spot project but they keep thinking of it as a *total* project."

And:

"The planners have to get out of their ivory tower and take a look at the city as it is. Take density—a great bugaboo as far as I'm concerned. What *are* the levels of density needed and supportable for a given neighborhood?

"The esthetics will come, but they should come second. No matter what you do—take our _____ project; we've got four great architects retained, but *somebody'll* be bound to come around later and say it looks like hell!"

From a friendlier point of view, one director pointed out that:

"The trouble with planners is that they don't get good liaisons with other agencies. They don't get to the good citizens' groups. And they don't relate their plans to any machinery for effectuating the plan— to carry it out. There are *real* conflicts of interest between business and the planning of a city."

And:

"One of the biggest areas of difficulty is the lack of political education at the local level. The program's drawn so much from planners, who are trained to hate politics, that it's weak politically. I can speak because I'm not a planner."

An official of URA explained some of this hostility of planners in these terms:

"The technicians look down on what the operations guys plan. They sit in the office and say, 'Why, you can't do that!' They don't look at

the problems out in the field—they look at their professional colleagues and say *you can't compromise!* that is, with reality."

The hostility to the content of the program which focuses upon the
planners, seems to derive from the basic nature of program organization. Urban renewal legislation and principles make no distinction
among cities and the Workable Program and project requirements
are supposed to apply to all alike. To protect the integrity of the program, it is necessary to check carefully each major decision beforehand against the rules set up by the Administration. The result is an
extreme degree of rigidity in principle, modified in an *ad hoc* fashion
as a response to local political conditions. The planners stand for the
Program's effort to apply a uniform set of standards to all American
cities:

Director: "You know, one thing that riles the aldermen is the lack
of autonomy the program gives you. This city is individual and it has
its own character. The federal government will look at a program we
think is good and they will be very doubtful about it. This upsets the
locals a lot.

[*A colleague*]: "Yes, but I have a little different interpretation. It
isn't the top guys who give us such a bad time, but the rank and file,
the technicians, who object to our program. And their detachment—
and downright ignorance—leads them to very arbitrary judgment."

Officials in a small city spoke of size and its effects:

"For one thing, there ought to be two distinct types [of program]—
one for the large urban area and one for communities under, say,
50,000. I would approach the two kinds quite differently.

Q: "What would be needed for smaller cities?

A: "Less requirements, less—

[*Colleague*]: "Regimentation?

A: "That's right! For instance, neighborhood analysis in a large
city is different from that in a small one. In Washington, D.C., you

have strong distinct types of areas, bounded and clear. But you don't have it here. It's primarily the same climate all down the street. You see, the whole program is suited to the 'Big Nine.'

Q: "Who?

A: "The biggest nine metropolitan areas. They control it from beginning to end and we have no say. But most of our programs are different and have to be different."

Region is also important when relocation is at issue. In some cities the housing choice is so small that urban renewal forces the construction of new public housing; in others,

"We're lucky. We can put them almost anywhere in the neighborhoods. There's a lot of residential integration. Then there's a lot of land and colored can buy—and builders will build as easy for colored as for white. We relocated them in better housing. The feds were concerned but we used a card-file system and they took cards at random and went out and looked at the families. It checked out."

In short, as one LPA official remarked, "Two plus two may be four anywhere, but I think I know better *what is two* in this town." What is two in this town sometimes refers to local norms, sometimes to local political power.

"We had a strip of highway, all paid for—but the feds objected to the price we paid. We paid too much! But we require higher standards of construction than most cities and we expect to pay for it. Then they didn't want to allow it as our contribution.

"They want us to adopt the American Public Health Association Housing Code—they don't care if urban renewal is destroyed in the process, our enemies organized and strengthened, or what. We have a code we can enforce now."

Political considerations are especially apt to be cited when URA gives the locals trouble over "citizen participation." In general, the strategy of the latter is to take support wherever it is offered and let sleeping dogs lie. URA's insistence upon a formal Citizen's Advisory Committee, as proper compliance with the "citizens participation" requirement, may be resented.

"We don't want one here—it would just be a divisive move, a way to organize your opposition. They say 'you've got one ready-made in [a local businessmen's group]' and l say the hell we have. We want them to be for us, and to do so they must be *completely unofficial.* The formal agency should take responsibility, and do the studies, and [the group] will organize the desire to see the work carried out and the downtown redeveloped."

Or:

"We already have a wide network of citizens' committees, but no formal Citizen's Advisory Committee. What do we tell all those other people when the URA insists upon one? It's an empty gesture, but it could cost us a real price."

The Urban Renewal Administration's increasingly vigorous efforts to protect those who are displaced by the projects has provoked serious criticism. The agency, in its anxiety for proper relocation, requires increasingly specific plans, then checks the results. One LPA official objected to the elaborate plans required beforehand:

"You know, they didn't need a detailed study of relocation needs for that little project for the university campus. Yet here it is, for thirty-six people with the one nonwhite separately tabulated all the way through. An expense of thousands of dollars."

And, in another city:

"On prediction—they make damned liars of you, forcing you to make statements nobody could make with any confidence. Like a detailed relocation plan. Hell, you can't tell what these people will and can do in eighteen months from now.

"My old buddy in the regional office used to come to me and say, 'What's the housing situation here?' I'd say, 'Look, here's our relocation plan.' He'd grin and say, 'Yeah, but tell me, what's the housing situation?' "

And:

"Relocation planning other than schematic outlines, done early in the steps of planning, is a waste of time. All that's useful is this question: Is a supply there and, if not, where will it come from?"

And:

"You know, you can write a beautiful story on where you're going to move people, but the beauty of our program is that we haven't moved people—we've helped them to move. The *flexibility* of the program has been the main virtue of it."

One official finally said, in a burst of impatience, "They've got to stop making a goddamned fetish out of relocation. It's terribly important, but we're devoting an inordinate amount of time to it." A great deal of that time is devoted, not to the thorny problems of convincing people they can and must upgrade their housing, but to convincing the URA that the local agency is serious about its relocation responsibilities.

It is clear that the effort to maintain careful control from the federal agency tends to slow the program at the local level. This occurs with relocation studies and with project feasibility studies. It is particularly apparent in the allocation of local improvements to project costs.

"For example, we're putting up a public parking facility two blocks away from the project and claim part of it as the city's contribution to the net cost of the project. They ask us: 'How much will it benefit the project?' And because you know you have to play patty-cake with them, you say, maybe seventy-five per cent. And the feds say fifty per cent, and then you bicker and play the endless bureaucratic game."

But it is apparent too in the insistence on local public responsibility:

"We need one particular parcel to complete a site. A church. They've agreed already on price and have it signed. But in the regional office it becomes a *cause célèbre*. The question is: Should we have another public hearing? Who'd be there? The bishop and me, that's who. A pure formality. But because of this—not because we have to have a hearing but because they can't decide whether we have to have one or not—we can't begin advertising that property, people can't plan —and it's already cleared except for the church!"

Requirements for fiscal planning become ever more difficult, as the time span of a project is lengthened. At last, plans collapse under the weight resulting from their overextension.

"You have to write up innumerable materials as supporting documents for a plan, and you're measuring *unknowns*. You're documenting an unknown plan to support a job six years henceforth and when you go out and make a budget of fiscal cost to a community, they're gonna have to change the cost later and they're gonna say, 'All those people out there in that office just gobble up federal dollars, that's all.' When we have to guess things we can't know and talk as if they were fact, we're making first-class liars out of ourselves.

Q: "What could be done about it?

A: "Well, we could at least say here's an anticipated budget, and use it for working purposes inside the agency—but don't publicize it as fact when it's just a set of rough assumptions.

[*Colleague*]: "That's where all the complications come in. All those studies up and down the line, hundreds of them, then you have to make it all work.

A: "Some of them are nothing in the world but planner's dreams."

Along the same vein:

"The big danger is that we get it so concretized that we defeat ourselves. Sometimes timing alone is of tremendous consequence, making the difference between failure and success. Your rules can throw timing way off. We've created this dilemma by our concern with being too precise."

And:

"If we have an orderly program—if people know what will happen over time—they'll go along with it with federal assistance.

Q: "Why is all this time-lag necessary?

A: "There's federal review, and federal re-review, and it takes a great deal of time. Not for us to propose, but for them to make up their minds.

[*Colleague*]: "When was the _____ Ward project started?

A: "In 1949, and still not one structure up."

The Regional Offices

The chief firing line in the URA is the regional office. This is where the LPA meets the control system of the federal agency, where major examinations and decisions are made, where the "technicians" sit in their offices, and where many of the locals center blame. Both procedures and personnel come in for some basic criticism.

"I think review of applications could be a little faster. We sent in an application; they said it was in good shape, yet it took seven months to get approval. *Yet they helped plan it and write it.* It's all spelled out pretty well, you know, even to get the planning advance. Ours had been in the regional office several months and I called and said, 'What gives?' and they told me, 'It's right here on the desk. We're just too swamped to even get at it.'"

Much of this is due to the simple shortage of trained personnel. Ironically, the regional office is competing with its own LPAs for officials.

"One of the toughest problems we've got is to get able guys on the staff. The stories I could tell you about men who work here one year and go out for $5,000 more to work for the cities I'm supervising! The top guys, the men I really want to hold responsible for, say [names very large cities] get top pay as GS12—that's $8,955. Do you wonder I lose my best guys? The local guys in the LPA may get two or three times that if they're good.

Q: "How does this come about? Bureau of Budget?

A: "Not entirely—internally we've had our own problems. It's been a technicians' program. It was small and the technical scales have always been higher than those for administrative heads. The technical guys start at $12,000. Then imagine my problem as an administrator—getting a GS12 to work on equal footing with the technicians.

Q: "Where do the field representatives come from?

A: "Out of the family of HHFA. Then the largest source has been the intern program. The agency puts a lot of stock in it and I'm a strong supporter, but when I came in here 90 per cent of the field representatives were young kids. Wonderful if you have some people who can train them, but you can't take a kid two years out of school and expect him to have the maturity of a man of forty. You send him to deal with mayors on a program as complicated as urban renewal—and yet the agency has relied on this!'"

Some of these field representatives were discussed by the LPA officials with whom they had to deal.

"I would hit another point. It would sound very minor to most people but it's a major thing, believe me. The HHFA cannot find the qualified type of help to act as what they call 'site representatives.' When they hire twenty-two-year-old kids to come and talk to a board about a multimillion-dollar deal, nobody trusts them."

And:

"I've already told the directors this. There's one thing I'd do. Get more trained and qualified technicians in the URA. Then drum it into their heads that it's a partnership instead of a contest between the Local Public Authority and the Urban Renewal Administration."

This particular criticism was repeatedly made. The shortage of trained officials means, in turn, that those who are capable must do double duty, checking the work of novices. This leads to the bottlenecks at the regional offices.

Much of the delay, however, is inevitable. The job as defined is close to impossible. The Workable Program is nothing less than an effort to revamp several agencies in each city, coordinate their work and, in the process, introduce a number of new and not very attractive tasks. Most of the housing codes passed by cities in the program were passed in response to the Workable Program requirement; they are radical innovations by administrative fiat. The program is a new departure for most municipal governments.

"I think that instead of setting up separate agencies in a local government and calling them commissions, then running them through a federal agency, you just have to get it away from the federal government. Because we *aren't* a local agency. We have to send everything to the regional office; they even tell you what you have to pay for the land, what you can sell it for—even the prices. Of course I know there'd be room for all kinds of collusion and sharp practice, but it's a lie now to call it a local program. It's federal."

The ambitious nature of the undertaking and the extremely weak control available through the formal requirements of the Workable Program lead some to see it as simply an educational effort. One official, more honest than some, assessed the program in these terms:

Q: "What of the Workable Program?

A: "We took them where they were and tried to bring them along as fast as they could be brought along. Now we have—what bothers me—built in rationally a rigidity in requirements that could threaten the whole program.

Q: "Could you give me an example?

A: "I think we're in that position in _____. The voters rejected the housing code. We've had several letters saying, 'We believe it is essential.' Therefore, no Workable Program, no 221D3 housing for them.

"But—are we in a better position to assist local government if we pick up our marbles and go home? I have to consider this seriously, because if we continue we may stop some other program cold.

"I'm interested in performance and not paperwork. You've got to have flexibility at the regional level. I've said it again and again, but they say, 'Yes, we understand, but you've got to stand up and be counted.'

"I say, 'Be counted over the body of a dying program?' It's unfair today to ask of Coos Bay what you ask of New Haven after New Haven's been in the business for a decade."

Slowing the local programs is only one side of the coin. Rigidity of requirements can have other effects. Patterned evasion of norms by local government can lead to dishonesty in the LPA and loss of integrity in the federal program.

"The Workable Program has turned into a monster. If you can get your local people to go along you can write anything you damned well want. Then if you're forced to it you end up making dishonest statements that help nobody. Then the requirement that it be approved by the City Council means here is a document that opens up a Pandora's box, that allows any dissident view to be expressed. Then the requirements mean you may slant the document a lot to get it through. This erodes the whole principle of what the Workable Program stands for."

And:

"It's admirable in principle, but the way they carry it out it's just a lot of hypocrisy [shows me the 'Report of Progress' under the WP]. I call it a Hypocritical Report of Progress."

And:

"When we started in here there were just three of us in this office. When the Workable Program requirement became law, I sat down and worked an hour; we complied with everything they wanted. We sent it in and never had any more trouble with them."

But (from the same official):

Q: "Is it just a bureaucratic control? Can you just give it lip-service and get by?

A: "I think you should comply. For those who don't, the URA should cut off the funds. I don't think the federal government should dump money into an area whether it's doing good or not."

And:

"It's an excellent tool—I'm one hundred per cent for it."

And:

"I think the Workable Program is one of the great contributions of the housing agencies in the last few years!"

What They Think Should Be Done

There are two diametrically opposed positions on the Workable Program, the "hard line" and the "soft line." The first requires a stringent enforcement of each requirement, with particular emphasis upon code enforcement and relocation, the two most difficult political tasks. Those who take this position have a powerful argument: Upon the Workable Program depends the entire rationale of urban renewal as an effort to eliminate and prevent slums and blight. If the main goals of the Workable Program cannot be achieved, if the standing stock of houses cannot be improved so that slum dwellers move to better housing, the remaining stock will be overcrowded and will deteriorate faster. So much for the logic of the hard line.

Everybody agrees with it in principle, but the nearer the LPA official is to the local agencies responsible, the more flexible his approach.

"Urban renewal should be handled similar to the community facility loans. The federal government should require that they set up their own local programs. Give them advice, but not strict requirements. Give them loans or grants, but strictly on a local basis—a real grant to the locality."

This is the extreme in the "soft line." A more general statement is this considered opinion from a regional official:

"We're short on services to *help* cities get services. We're very long on bludgeoning and criticizing them. If we're continually asked for follow-up studies, it must take time from our other work—maybe more useful work.

"Cities are new at this game. We've got to develop resources. We have to talk to builders, realtors, councilmen, lenders—not spend all of our time investigating the houses people are in now!"

The more forcefully the federal agency presses its Workable Program, the more explosive are the political reactions in the local community. These political backfires, in turn, illuminate the magnitude of the social changes that are supposed to be brought about by the Program. The result is a heavy emphasis upon urban renewal as a kind of extension program, a teaching and persuading device, to help city officials understand their problems, the Workable Program as a solution to them, and ways of effecting that program.

"Let me get one big major point across. I left it to last and it's the biggest. To accomplish urban renewal the problem we have to cope with is this. When you take anything as complex as urban renewal you can't explain it to people, and that's what's causing all the defeat of urban renewal in the United States.

"Trouble is a few people, who've seen what happens in South America, where there aren't any middle classes and the very wealthy and very poor are all (and the poor have no say on urban renewal), come back here and try it and it doesn't work—because people can protest. If I were trying to revamp it I would certainly try to make it easier for the people to digest."

This man had recently suffered a series of political defeats. However, in another city, with a flourishing program, the educational emphasis was equally strong.

"The answer to the whole thing is in planning, the revision of codes and enforcement of codes, and, especially—*broad public education*. Tell them how to 'make our city beautiful.' There's not enough evidence yet of what urban renewal can do, but people already realize the stimulus that projects give to surrounding areas. I think we'll reach the day when we've reduced blight to a minimum, and then can stay with it."

Another official was much less concerned with the general citizenry, and more concerned with the supposed targets of the program, the residents in blighted areas. His concern stemmed from difficulties in relocation and code enforcement:

"Something has to be done about organizing these urban neighborhoods. Out of this sort of work has got to come community awareness of what the city is—that it's theirs, what the problems are and the tools available. Few people know who to call on complaints. Surprisingly, those who do get prompt service. The mass doesn't know or have any faith. This is going to take *education*."

These quotations underscore the novelty of the program and the feeling of isolation from broad social norms, understood and accepted by the population. Education is necessary for the specific steps in the program; it is necessary for long-term political support in the community and nation. But what kind of program needs this support? What are the aims of the LPA directors, the housers and planners and rebuilders of cities?

Officials Talk of Goals

Urban renewal is a tool that can be used for a wide variety of tasks. It can be used to renew banks, to build tall buildings in the CBD where only pawnshops and tattoo parlors stood before. It can be used to keep Negroes out of threatened neighborhoods. It can also be used to rehabilitate mixed neighborhoods, leaving them clean, standard, and still ethnically "integrated." It can be used for various purposes, public and private.

Some programs are being used for public improvements in the slums:

"All the same, I'd like to show the critics some of these small southern cities. These places are really using urban renewal money to pave and sewer the Negro quarters, to start improving their physical plant *for the first time in history.*"

And some LPA officials are primarily oriented to providing alternatives to slums for the citizens of their towns. When one was asked what he thought the program should do, his answer was short: "Produce more low-cost housing." Such answers were rare, however. As a Negro official in a city with thousands of Negroes on the waiting list for public housing said: "No, sir. It's aimed at central city build-up. You can't sell it here as housing."

And this was the common focus of attention: the "central city build-up."

Q: "Do you really need urban renewal? Why?
A: "Yes sir. For instance, this street here should be the central business district. It once was. But now look at it. One man can't redevelop one building and make sense—it has to be a community project. So instead, they move away, leasing us this property. The guy across the street demolished one old building; he makes more on the space as a parking lot. Urban renewal in this area would be justified by your tax increase alone."

And:

"Our CBD project is cheek by jowl with the central financial and administrative area. It will be redeveloped with a complex of high- and low-rise residential structures. It will also provide five commercial blocks as a reserve for the central financial district—2,000,000 square feet of office space!"

And:

"I think there are great possibilities for residential renewal for the inner city. You see it going on in Philadelphia and you see it in Los Angeles. I suppose it's a question of how you buffer areas, change codes for conversion—how you deal with accusations that are thrown about for corraling certain minority groups."

The open-ended definition of the program leads to some truly global aims. Starting with the slum clearance program of 1937, modest and limited, the urban renewal program today represents a general attack on everything to some of its protagonists:

"It should do whatever is necessary in the local community to overcome problems that, without it, wouldn't be overcome.
Q: "How do you decide what is necessary?
A: "Different communities have different problems. There could be a city that needs most of all a monument. In another city the

most important thing may be to clean out something so terrible that cleaning it out—even to open land if there's no other need—is still worth doing. I don't object to getting away from a housing program. The more flexible we are the more effective we'll be in tackling the individual problems of the community. Every problem we uncover has ganglions into many corners of the community. This is why so many things have been tacked on."

For those who are still concerned with residential blight, or slums, the program opens up indefinitely:

"The project allowed us to take an inventory of housing. In the process we took an inventory of all the social problems of slums. People often blamed us for the social problems! We had to say, 'Look, we didn't do it.' In one household we found two generations of unwed mothers, with twenty-one children altogether.

Q: "What did you do?

A: "We put them in a house and watched them for a year—but we were too easy on them. We ended up having a hell of a time getting rid of them—and they'd do nothing to improve their position. Now we're talking about the experimental segregation of all the problem families [i.e., from public housing] in housing especially administered."

Such concern is logical, if slums result from poverty and if poverty results from "social problems." Two "housers" were asked why they were concerned with housing:

"Next time I hear the phrase, 'our American way of life,' I'll scream. What is it? And 'private enterprise'? They're all for government subsidy to the fast buck. You're inviting Communism when a fourteen-year-old girl, like one in my neighborhood last week, is taken to a hospital for severe malnutrition.

"I have an old-fashioned ideal. Democracy should work for everybody. I'm not going to change it either; I'm going to try to make it work. I want us to say there *is* an American way of life. I see people living in a condition that doesn't support the dignity of a human life and I don't believe in it and I'm trying to do something about it."

And:

"Well, we argue this and that. Because people are interested in the payoff for them, I tell them, I tell an assessor—he isn't interested in anything except there'll be a lot of assessment business.

"But when you get down to it, we want to get people into better shape, so they can live better lives."

The more broadly the program is conceived, the more vague and general become the terms in which it is described. In one city, with projects ranging from slum clearance to downtown renovation, university campus expansion to public housing, an official put it this way:

"Fundamentally, I think renewal ought to be used as the device by which you seek to mobilize every available resource in the community from a political and economic and social standpoint to do whatever may be required to provide a better urban climate.

"The local public authority is, hopefully, a catalyst to bring this about. You can't take on one job at a time—it's a hopeless strategy. Your dynamics will overtake you. You've also got to take the curse off—that urban renewal is done only when something is bad. You've got to try to get something for everyone.

"If only there could be acceptance that the urban renewal approach is in effect never-ending, not just a concentrated initial task but a means of constantly updating, looking at promise and practice in the program, continually adjusting."

Another official agreed with the last point, but differed sharply in the range of ambitions an urban renewal program should espouse:

"You don't aim at rehabilitation—it's a fixation. Instead, we want constant maintenance. We're experimenting with the proportion of public investment that will spark a given amount of private investment in a given place, used to maintain the plant at a given level. Urban renewal should be a way of programing public capital investment for areas that need renewal, conservation, rehabilitation, and the like.

"You can't get at everything. You must focus. Otherwise your studies end up as a pile of crap, or a massive pile of data on the community in general which the community doesn't understand.

"These programs, as they age, add factors that seem relevant, factor after factor, until you end up with efforts to handle the whole damned universe and you just can't do it!"

The urban renewal program may also be seen as a series of experiments in community development and redevelopment.

"I think you've got to start with the assumption that you've got dozens of different situations. Each LPA is struggling to handle its problems in its situation, and they differ. St. Louis, Little Rock, Milwaukee, all are different. I think each may work out a good method, but different. Maybe in another decade or so we'll have a really dependable and effective tool to build our cities with. Maybe by the year 2,000 we'll have licked the slums."

Another, more cynical observer, put the same proposition in a different way:

"Look, your community is whatever your political structure will let you get done. The community makes up its mind. It's like your wife when she buys a new dress. How does she do it? I don't know, but the main thing is she did it. Maybe it's a lousy decision, but—so she made a mistake! Whatever mechanism you've got to make a decision the community makes up its mind and you have to work with it.

Q: "What do you mean by a 'lousy decision'?

A: "Good is what cities want to make themselves into; some cities are shallow in their notion of what's good—some just want to grow.

This is the way most people think. They're not very smart about it. They just want to make a buck.

Q: "What is the long-run possibility that urban renewal *can* work for the city as a whole?

A: "We have actually got to start planning for new metropolitan areas. You just can't make L.A. or Chicago an effective city. It isn't possible. We're lucky that, in our infinite unreason, we didn't make another Tokyo.

"Why, you drive on that [express highway] at rush hour and it's almost more than your nerves can stand. You can't just go on, adding more and more to it. We've got to think about planning some new metropolitan areas."

Summary: Urban Renewal as Social Organization

The urban renewal program has accumulated, over the twenty-five years since the Housing Act of 1937, three different sets of aims. First, and hallowed by age if not by effectiveness, is the goal of a "decent home and a suitable environment" for every American family; that is, replacement of slums by standard housing. Second is the goal of redeveloping the central city and, particularly, the central business district. Finally, as a result of deep uncertainty concerning the effects of spot redevelopment and rehabilitation, the program has developed the general goal of the planned city based upon a community renewal program.

Such goals are not necessarily contradictory. In fact, the last is supposed to integrate the other two. However, they are not identical. As we have noted earlier, *blight* may be so defined as to leave *slums* extant, and vice versa.[6] And either commercial blight removal in the CBD or slum elimination in the gray areas may progress without any

6 See Chapter 2.

general community renewal plan. Thus the LPA has a wide range of alternatives in its choice of project sites and goals. In trying to understand how it is that particular buildings are destroyed in some areas of a city, it is useful to look at the LPA as a social organization, deeply committed to the local community on one hand, to URA on the other.

Because of the widespread American belief that local autonomy is sacred, that local agents know better "what is two in this town," and that local commitment is therefore necessary, the projects are locally initiated. This is of basic importance to the entire program, for it is the localities that propose; the URA can only dispose. Its disposal is frequently late in the game, after a complex chain of events has developed a tentative consensus in the local polity. Thus the decision may be between *this* project and *no* project. The federal agency, however, has no very dependable guide for evaluating proposed projects anyway; it may suspect that a given project will not "work" in terms of short-run financial considerations, but there is no theory of slum causation and CBD withering away that would allow evaluation beyond such suspicions. Thus the agency falls back upon its Workable Program requirements and accepts a wide variety of local efforts. But it should be reemphasized that the program, as written in the law, simply *does not offer clear priorities.*

When two or more widely differing aims are allocated to the same social organization, particularly if the basic logic of these aims is not congruent, that organization appears opportunistic and lacking in integrity. The LPA suffers from this condition. This is accentuated by the weakness of our theory about urban social change, and the confusion of two kinds of propositions: (1) those that have to do with the "goodness" or "badness" of given conditions, and, (2) those that have to do with fact and cause. Many of the basic decisions made in the LPAs are based upon the first kind of judgment: Where is the "blighted" area to be redeveloped, which "slum" is to be cleared?

These are pejorative judgments, of land use and of housing conditions. We have noted their essentially administrative nature—they are facts by fiat. Codified in standards, they reflect the norms and values of the standard-makers and not necessarily any broad consensus in the community, certainly not the opinions of those who work or live there. Housing codes have no necessary relationship to the norms held by those who live in neighborhoods judged substandard; their neighborhood norms are internally produced and validated among their equals. The Negroes of Hyde Park-Kenwood felt, with justification, that the neighborhoods were excellent, relative to their alternative choices. But, since the LPA has no theory that would direct action to Hyde Park-Kenwood on the basis of maximal social benefits as compared to alternative action, its decisions are produced by the grounds of consensus in the larger, political, community.

The _effective_ grounds of consensus in any community are the decisions of those groups whose support is necessary for the LPA to stay in business. Therefore the "local community" is heavily biased toward those who control political power and community approval, on the one hand, and those who control credit and building development on the other. The LPA needs a market for its cleared land; it needs capital for the local contribution; it needs political support for the authoritative actions the local governors must take. (In one city, sixty-two separate council actions were necessary for one small project.) To aggregate consent among these scattered groups requires a program tailored to their needs and norms.

As a result, the residents of the declining neighborhoods have very little weight in the decisions. Banfield and Wilson note that, "Only rarely, if ever, has the opposition of slum dwellers prevented a redevelopment project anywhere once it has been seriously proposed."[7] These are usually neighborhoods of the bottom dogs; they lack expertise, organizational skills, and association with the powerful. The local interests represented are usually quite alien to those people most immediately affected.

Pointing out the lack of information, as well as lack of organizational competence among the Boston West Enders, Gans finally concludes:

[7] In _City Politics in America_, Chap. XX (in manuscript).

The truth was, that for a group unaccustomed to organizational activity, saving the West End was an overwhelming, and perhaps impossible, task. Indeed, there was relatively little the Committee could do. The decision had been made early in the decade, and it had received the blessings of the city's decisive business leaders and politicians. The West End's local politicians all opposed the redevelopment, but were powerless against the unanimity of those who favored it.[8]

Burd details the long and unsuccessful struggle of Mrs. Scala, a leader of the Harrison-Halstead area, to prevent its demolition; again, she was utterly ineffectual against the coalition of Chicago leaders who found the area the solution to their problems. Referring to the final shape of the Hyde Park-Kenwood redevelopment plan, Rossi and Dentler observe the coerciveness of the chain of events:

> . . . the administrative machinery surrounding urban renewal did not provide means for the participation of metropolitan groups until the very last stages. . . . Furthermore, the City Council was not empowered to do more than give blanket endorsement or rejection of the Plan. [235] [And], The effect of such last minute opposition is to draw together the former antagonists into a solid front and to arouse suspicions about the motives of the latecomer. [238][9]

In Newark, as in Chicago, Kaplan observed the development (through private negotiations) of a "non-amendable package" that was presented as a *fait accompli* to the residents in areas to be cleared, as well as the remainder of the citizenry.

Then the three relevant components of the "local community" are the LPA, the local governing body, and the business interests concerned with redevelopment. There is intense interaction among the three classes, over a long period of time, when the settlement is under negotiation. The LPA is usually weakest, since it is overwhelmingly committed to action, while such action may be only

---

[8] Gans, *The Urban Villagers*, p. 298.
[9] *The Politics of Urban Renewal*, pp. indicated in actual quotations. For the Harrison-Halstead opposition, see Burd, "Press Coverage."

marginally attractive to political, financial, or civic leaders. As a consequence, the LPA director becomes, willy-nilly, a public entrepreneur, an operator who makes the public business of urban renewal his private business. Aided by local civic leaders and, in the more successful programs, by a powerful elected political leader, he defines his program, but only in terms acceptable to his supporters.[10] These are a relatively small proportion of the organized and powerful groups in the city. In fact, the city can be divided into (1) those who want renewal, (2) those who do not care about renewal but do care about protecting other interests that may be affected, (3) those who do not know *or* care at all (most citizens), and (4) those who will care most but have the least say.

The consequence is a program that rewards the strong and punishes the weak. Accepting support where it is available, the LPA also tailors its program to the desires of those with an interest in "reviving downtown," the central business district. These turn out to be mayors concerned with increasing the central city tax base, civic leaders with a patriotic desire to "make our city center beautiful," businessmen with deep commitments to downtown real estate, and those who believe government should innovate in the public interest. For:

> The urban renewal slogan has proved to be a clarion call to everyone within hearing distance, and an omnibus for all wayfarers, night crawlers, social workers, and city planners. Its sex appeal is simple: It has allowed a new start.[11]

The "new start" represents a summing up of the interests of this heterogeneous group, weighted by their independent power and their commitment to showing accomplishment in a tangible form. Thus there is very little that is new about the start. The radical proposal

---

[10] Cf., for many case studies, George Duggar and others, *Local Organization for Urban Renewal in the United States* (Berkeley: University of California Bureau of Public Administration, preliminary reading copy, n.d.).

[11] Dean Swartzel, as quoted by George S. Duggar, "The Politics of Urban Renewal: Suggestions for a Conceptual Scheme" (St. Louis: American Political Science Association, paper, September 1961).

that housing be brought up to a certain standard by the use of the police power is ignored; the older order, wherein the CBD should be the center and symbolic hub of the metropolitan community, is shored up with public funds and the right of eminent domain.

Nor is this surprising. The local programs reflect the city as it is, a loose congeries of organized and segmented groups. Each LPA is concerned with its own interests—to attain funds, change land use, and thereby show cause for existence. In the process, it reinforces the existing system. Discussing the net loss of low-cost housing in Hyde Park-Kenwood, Rossi and Dentler concluded:

> . . . as proponents worked to build widespread support for the plan, the most controversial features of the program had to be eliminated. The program had to become big enough, but *bland* enough, to attract powerful supporters.[12]

Or, as the informant quoted earlier would have it, "Your community is whatever your political structure will let you get done."

[12] Rossi and Dentler, *Politics of Urban Renewal*, p. 64.

Chapter 6

THE PROGRAM IN THE LIGHT OF SOCIAL TRENDS

Urban renewal as an action program aims to change the existing cityscape. To be complete, it must also modify the processes resulting in unwanted aspects of the cities. Such intervention requires a realistic notion of the broad, ongoing regularities in social behavior which produce these aspects: We must know what the trends are, their magnitude, and their rigidity. Against this body of knowledge we can then measure urban renewal as a tool.

Any social action program must exist within a cage of constraints that it did not produce and cannot dissolve. When the massive regularities making up that cage can be identified as basic to a program's objectives they must be taken into account intellectually, for they will most certainly arise as "problems" in achieving these objectives. Hopefully, the program may be a catalyst for change in the broader picture; pessimistically, if it cannot, it will be either irrelevant to, or bent in the direction of, the overriding forces.

The program of urban redevelopment and urban renewal, originating in 1949, was twelve years old by December 1961. The total expenditures to that date were $2,481,103,000.[1] This sounds like a huge sum of money, until we remember that the private building industry averaged around ten billion dollars *a year* during this same period, as did the private rehabilitation and maintenance industry. Measured thus, by crude dollars, the Urban Renewal Administration committed its controlled dollars in the ratio of about one to every 120 free-market dollars. This is rather like controlling an elephant with a toothpick.

Vernon, speaking of the urban renewal program in New York City, put it in these terms:

> In New York City itself, renewal projects of heroic proportions have been developed during the past twenty years, involving public funds in various ways. The programs have affected a considerable number of people: over 85,000 dwelling units were built between 1946 and 1957, and nearly 500,000 people are housed in these structures. Yet, all told, the effects of these programs on land use in the City have been astonishingly small. The land area these projects occupy is not much over two square miles. In Manhattan, Brooklyn, and the Bronx, where renewal has made the greatest progress, only 1.4 per cent of the total land area has been involved.[2]

This is the local program that envious LPA officials elsewhere see as getting the lion's share of CBD renewal funds. But informed estimates of the area of "blight" in New York City range between five and ten times the areas treated to date.[3] For the nation as a whole, however, the program has moved much more slowly; only 47 urban renewal projects had been completed by 1961, while 518 were in process of execution. This only indicates that the program has been slow in gaining approval. To estimate its final effectiveness it is necessary to look at the cage of constraints, stemming from broad social trends, within which it must operate.

[1] *Report of Urban Renewal Operations,* Table I.

[2] Raymond Vernon, *Metropolis 1985* (Cambridge: Harvard University Press, 1960), p. 142.

[3] See Robert C. Wood, *1400 Governments* (Cambridge: Harvard University Press, 1961), and Banfield and Wilson, *City Politics* (Cambridge: Harvard University Press, 1963).

Trends Producing Urban Renewal

The urban renewal program is a response to a social problem that has been defined as a legitimate concern of government. And, as Robert A. Nisbet remarks, "the popular view of social problems likens them to cancers: for most citizens, the image of society and its problems is that of an essentially healthy organism invaded by alien substances." [4]

Such a naive view, resting on the unfounded analogy between organism and society, leads one to try to cure the "cancer" without considering the conditions of a society that caused it. The more useful approach would emphasize the inescapable nature of social problems: In a society such as ours they are handmaidens and children of broad social change. As I have noted elsewhere:

> Such change is continually vitiating the old assumptions of what is normal, right, and to be expected. The situations men face are not adequately handled by their socially inherited definition, and stable parts of the social environment become indeterminate and problematical. Out of collective definitions and collective choice comes an unanticipated world of new regularities, some of which violate old expectations and are seen as problems. [5]

When such problems engage the interests and attentions of the politically effective, they are translated into problems of the polity. Thus it is important, in analyzing urban renewal, to ask: What is the problem? To whom is it a problem? How did the problematic situation come about? In the light of answers to these questions we may then usefully ask: How appropriate is this action program as a response?

---

[4] Robert K. Merton and Robert A. Nisbet, eds., *Contemporary Social Problems* (New York: Harcourt-Brace, 1961), p. 10.

[5] "Traffic, Transportation, and the Problems of the Metropolis," in Merton and Nisbet, *ibid.*, p. 623.

The "problem" addressed seems to inhere in two separate and dramatic sets of circumstances. The first is, simply, the persistence in a prosperous economy of large neighborhoods of substandard housing in central cities. The second is the relative decline of the central business district in the economic life of the metropolitan area. They may be connected, if it is thought that the first produces the second (or vice versa), but they really have different origins and are important to different sets of people.

The program to provide a "decent home and suitable environment for every American family" has its roots, as noted earlier, in the New Deal. The present importance of housing in urban renewal still rests upon the older period when it was believed that "one third of a nation" was ill-housed. Today this is far from true by most standards, but governmental responsibility for housing has been rather firmly established. It is part of the agenda, its bureaucracy is venerable (and has even been accepted for cabinet status), and it is accepted by the citizenry. Though many criticize specific policies, few people fight hard to "get the government out of the housing business"; even the National Association of Real Estate Boards has found it possible to endorse federal programs, while the Eisenhower Administration passed the major 1954 housing bill. Those who are most concerned with housing, however, tend to be old warhorses from the New Deal —union leaders, ethnic leaders, welfare organizations—in short, liberals concerned with distributing the income in such a way as to improve the share of the poor.[6]

---

[6] "Those supporting the [1949] bill included the American Association of Social Workers, American Association of University Women, American Federation of Labor, American Public Health Association, American Veterans of World War II, (AMVETS), Congress of Industrial Organizations, Federal Council of Churches of Christ in America, National Association of Housing Officials, National Board of the Young Women's Christian Association, National Council of Jewish Women, National Institute of Municipal Law Officers, United States Conference of Mayors, and Veterans of Foreign Wars of the United States." (Foard and Fefferman, "Legislation," p. 643n.) Many of these may have been more concerned with redevelopment than housing. An interesting indication of the "hard-core housers" is the list of groups who opposed the Hyde Park-Kenwood renewal bill in the Chicago City Council because of its detrimental effect on ethnic and low-cost housing. These included the Urban League, the National Association for the Advancement of Colored People, the Cardinal's Committee on Conservation, the Communist Party of Illinois, the Tenants and Home Owners Association (a Hyde Park-Kenwood

The problem of the central city enlists another array of support. The problematic situation here is the decline of the central business district as its residential hinterland is occupied by the ethnic and the poor, while suburban shopping centers take most of the lucrative new market and some of the older market. As downtown streets change from quality shopping to bargain shopping, from bargain shopping to "skid row," the property declines in value. So does the tax base. Thus tax rates will have to go up, or else the public services may decline. Higher taxes or poor services in turn make the city less attractive for new enterprise—a vicious circle. Those who identify this as a serious problem are committed to the central city. They include those with financial interests in the center, those with political interests in the central city electorate, those with governmental responsibility for the central city, and all those for whom the city is hub and symbolic center of the metropolitan community.[7]

Each of these socially problematic situations arose from the continuous process of change endemic to our urban complexes. Those who identify them as problems have often contributed to their creation—as in the central-city property owners who live in the suburbs, or liberals who supported legislation that only underwrites housing for the middle-income classes. Now they wish to change the powerful flow of housing distribution and urban location. To do so, one must understand how these came about, for here is the origin of the central city's "problem."

---

group), the C.I.O. Cook County Industrial Union Council, the Chicago Institute of Social Welfare, the United Packinghouse Workers Union, and five community organizations from other parts of the city. (Rossi and Dentler, *Politics of Urban Renewal,* p. 269.)

[7] "There is still a strong belief among many in Congress that the principal objective of the urban renewal program is the removal of slums and the improvement of housing, as distinguished from general city betterment. On the other side are the municipalities and local officials, ably represented in Congress and before its committees, who want more discretion in planning and deciding the type of projects to be undertaken. An added force which seems to be tipping the balance in their favor is *the position of business interests which normally tend to support restrictions on federal expenditures, but are increasingly in favor of reconstructing blighted business and industrial properties.*" [My italics.] (Foard and Fefferman, "Legislation," pp. 671–672.) In the Hyde Park-Kenwood battle over housing in the renewal agency, the mortgage bankers, City Hall, and the University of Chicago exercised great leverage on the City Council to approve a plan with no low-cost and little middle-cost housing. (Rossi and Dentler, *Politics of Urban Renewal,* esp. Chap. 9.)

The Changing Space-Time Ratio

Urban complexes are possible and necessary because of a widespread integration of human activities. The city that developed in the nineteenth century was supported by growing networks of rail that integrated local, regional, and national economies. Within the city, however, integration is also crucial, and in the older cities of the steam age such integration was possible only through animal muscles, human and equine. Thus the nineteenth century saw a giantism of urban complexes but great density within each complex, for movement was slow and difficult and therefore minimized by crowding sites close together. Near the terminals of rail and steamship lines the heavy industry centered; nearby was the dense housing of the industrial work force.

First the street railway, then the automobile, radically lowered the time-cost for movement within the urban complex. This allowed the integration of activities over wider geographical space at the same cost in time as before. The net result was an increase in *locational freedom*. This freedom applied to all who had the resources necessary to command the newer methods of movement.

It applied most spectacularly to the location of residences. The automobile suddenly created an enormous new peripheral area that could be used as housing for the city workers. With the new residential neighborhoods came the stores, then the complexes of stores, and finally the rationally planned suburban shopping centers. The latter, using undeveloped land in large parcels, could provide an esthetic attractiveness and convenience that are hard to come by in the inherited welter of land use common to the central business district.

As market and residential areas moved outward, so did the jobs. Industry oriented to the market, to the white-collar and skilled labor force, began to move after. As the distribution of retail sales shifted outward, warehouses and truck terminals found it useful to halve the distance from center to periphery—they moved toward the outer central city or to the giant circumferential roads around the suburban rings. And, perhaps most importantly, industry that required (as with the shopping center) large tracts of clear land moved toward the outskirts where such land was available. Trucks and rail spurs obviated the earlier need for proximity to the rail terminal.

The results are familiar. The residential tract development, the suburban shopping center, the industrial park, all new since 1920, are household words for students of the city today. They are all ways of exploiting greater locational freedom. With such freedom, centrality loses its former value and the central city, an enormous plant built to the specifications of the age of steam, ceases to grow. For it could have grown only through a more intensive use of land, through density and high-rise structures. Such structures, however, do not fit either the residential requirements of the population or the needs of the horizontal, continuous-flow factories; with the rise of the automobile there is no necessity for them. Thus our central cities remain constant or decline in population and economic activity, while the areas outside their boundaries develop rapidly, and horizontally.

The Changing Population

During the period of the automobile revolution other massive changes were occurring in the characteristics of the urban population. At the turn of the century America's large cities were half-ethnic: Minority citizens from Russia, Germany, Italy, Africa, Poland, Ireland made up half of the total. They were also cities of the poor; the average income in real dollars was half that of today. And they were cities where the average man lived in an apartment—a tenement or town house. Acculturation to and success in such cities were associated with smaller families, lower fertility. Such a city was the ideal typical "mosaic of worlds that touch but do not interpenetrate" identified by early human ecologists. There were the ethnic worlds of the ghetto, the Chinatown, the Polish district, class worlds of skid row, the slum, the "gold Coast" and the hobohemia, worlds separated by life style —the urbane world of the "upper bohemians" and "society," the peasant world of the villagers transplanted to Boston or Chicago.

In general, however, these differentia were correlated. The ethnic newcomers, with their broken English, were also the poor who lived a transplanted half-peasant life. The "old Americans" were more prosperous, more literate, more "honorably" employed; they controlled birth and had smaller families. Today these correlations have broken down. The children and grandchildren of the immigrants are indistinguishable from one another and from the "old Americans"; the increasing wealth of the society has meant that the average income is double that of 1900 and, as this occurs, there is greater variation by commitments and life style.[8]

For the purpose of this essay, the main thing that has occurred is an increase in social choice, distributed over a wide range of the population. Segregation is a function of ethnic identity and social class: As ethnics acculturate and income rises, they are able to leave their "mosaics" and enter the general labor and housing markets. All have not achieved such freedom, of course. There remain the very poor and those ethnics against whom the barriers are still very rigid —the colored residents. However, even though their numbers have increased greatly as the expanding labor force drew them from Mexico, Puerto Rico, and the South, they are today an absolute minority in a world of the nonsegregated.

The Changing Governmental Structure

As the population spread outside the governmental walls of the city, residential enclaves incorporated themselves as municipal units. For a time such units were annexed by the central city, when its own urbanized fringes merged with theirs, but during the 1920's such annexation came to a halt. In the beginning this was often due to

[8] For a more extended and systematic discussion, see Scott Greer, *The Emerging City* (New York: The Free Press, 1962).

resistance from the city government, which would have to supply expensive services to residential areas that were "tax losses." Later, though, the residents of suburban municipalities came to value the governmental walls as a means of controlling their own fate—their land use, their neighbors, and their public treasury with its uses. As services were developed for the suburbs, the central cities had little to offer as inducements to merge, while in state legislatures the suburban and rural legislators united in making forced annexation by the city impossible.

One major reason for the attrition of the annexation process was, undoubtedly, the differences between suburban and central city populations. The governmental walls were a way of expressing and maintaining such differences. Though suburbs rose to municipality status for many reasons (some had no other means of supplying basic utilities, some were tax shelters for industry, some were shelters for gambling and other prohibited entertainment), once in being they became rigid entities, separating neighborhood from neighborhood and, more important, all suburbia *en masse* from the central city.[9]

Thus the urban complexes have experienced increasing freedom in location together with an increasing freedom of social choice for most households, but a decreasing freedom to suburbia *as a whole*. The most dramatic effect of the changes, taken altogether, has been a splintering of political power, a fractionation of the polity, which makes action for the metropolis as a whole impossible.

The Output: Segregation by Land Use and Government

The increasing freedom of choice for the urban population has led it, overwhelmingly, to choose the single-family dwelling unit. After World War II the federal government, through its mortgage insurance programs, made the ownership of new, single-family dwelling units

[9] For further discussion, including an analysis of suburban politics, see Scott Greer, *Governing the Metropolis* (New York: John Wiley and Sons, 1962).

extremely easy. The FHA and VA programs produced lower down-payments and longer periods of loan (thus lower monthly payments) through guaranteeing loans, so that no risk remained to the investor. The HHFA has been severely criticized for this policy, yet there seems little doubt that most Americans with freedom to choose want the owner-occupied, single-family unit. Survey after survey indicates that some 90 per cent agree it is best to own such a home.[10]

Such homes can only be built in the peripheral areas. The land cost in the built-up city is prohibitive for unsubsidized units of this sort. Thus the freedom of choice resulting from increasing social rank and acculturation, together with the locational freedom allowed by the auto, resulted in an option for the suburban house in the tract development. There is little indication of dissatisfaction with such homes once they are bought: Neither the distance to work nor the loss of central-city cultural facilities are important to the new suburbanites. In fact, they are much more apt to be satisfied with their choice than are those remaining in the older central city.[11]

The two programs subsidizing the housing industry, FHA and VA, have been administered through private lending agencies. They are essentially insurance schemes that guarantee mortgages. Through their commitment to private agencies they have shored up the preferences of private lenders—for *new* houses, for *single-family* houses, for *younger* families and for *white* families. In this way they have been discriminatory against those whose preferences vary from the mode, who want more urban living, in older, multiple-unit structures, in older parts of the city. They have also discriminated against those with unusual problems and greater needs, the older house-seeker and

---

[10] For example, see Theodore Caplow, "Home Ownership and Location Preferences in a Minneapolis Sample." *American Sociological Review* Vol. VIII, No. 6 (December 1948), pp. 725–730; Herbert Gans, "Urbanism and Suburbanism as Ways of Life: A re-evaluation of Definitions" in *Human Behavior and Social Processes,* ed. Arnold M. Rose (Boston: Houghton-Mifflin Company, 1962); Janet Abu-Lughod and Mary Mix Foley in *Housing Choices and Constraints,* ed. Martin Meyerson (New York: McGraw-Hill Book Company, Inc., 1960).

[11] See *ibid.,* as well as Scott Greer and Ella Kube, "Urbanism and Social Structure" in *Community Structure and Analysis,* ed. Marvin Sussman (New York: Thomas Y. Crowell and Co., 1959).

the Negro population. Since the programs are public subsidies, one may question their equity on these grounds.

But a major reason *for the competitive advantage of suburbia* is that the housing of the central city, built in a day of less locational freedom, is dense and old. It is largely multiple-family and there is little private outdoor space. Thus it declines in value and is rented to those who can get no other housing—either because of poverty or because of their ethnic identity. In brief, the central city, particularly the inner area (first built and most obsolete, in automobile-day terms), is increasingly the home of the workingman's family and the segregated ethnics. Meanwhile suburbia becomes less exclusive, comes to include the wide middle range of urban population as well as the exurban wealthy. Farthest out on the fringe are the shacktowns, the unincorporated settlements of the poor. They have little effect on the middle-class suburbs because of governmental boundaries. The central city distribution, however, is heavily loaded with recently arrived ethnics and the poor, and they are electorate, taxpayer, and resident.

Such populations are apt to be greater tax losses than the middle ranks whom they replace. Welfare, police, the entire range of tax-supported services, are more expensive for them, while their low income makes them poor tax sources. At the same time the central business district, once the major market for the metropolitan population, becomes the convenience shopping center for the poor.[12] This leads to changes of merchandise offered and merchandising methods, which together discourage "quality" trade. Thus structures are not renovated or replaced, and the commercial tax base declines. Finally, as industrial firms need new plant space, they may very well choose the suburban industrial park or even move their old plant there for a new start; the old plant is apt to be deteriorating, obsolete, and landlocked. Then commercial and residential decline is not replaced by industrial shifts: The chief growing use in the central area is public and nonprofit—hospitals, colleges, express highways—tax-exempt properties that are net losers.

[12] Cf., C. T. Jonassen, *The Shopping Center Versus Downtown* (Bureau of Business Research, College of Commerce and Administration, Ohio State University, 1955).

In short, the changes brought about by greater locational freedom and greater social choice have resulted in the "trickling down" of the central city plant on the continuum of values. Housing no longer desired by the white middle class is handed on to lower-income populations; stores and plants no longer desired by prosperous growing enterprises are handed on to marginal enterprises. Rents decline as this occurs, and taxes are apt to decline with them. Declining taxes, in turn, lead to declining public services—which feed back upon the general desirability of the property. For the individual owner, maintenance is an increasing proportion of rents; for the city government, maintenance is an increasing proportion of taxes. The cost of maintenance tends to increase with age, while taxes and rents decline.

As the input of social capital in the form of money and energy declines, the neighborhoods of the wealthy, the prosperous, and the "decent" become neighborhoods of the poor. Buildings are painted less frequently, streets remain littered, street lights are broken and not replaced, and the police avoid the area. The story is repeated in Morningside Heights and Hyde Park-Kenwood, as well as in hundreds of lesser-known neighborhoods. In the CBD the exclusive shops give way to mass department stores patronized by Negroes, to discount houses and chili parlors, to a working-class bazaar. It is a logical product of a free market in land and housing, disproportionately concentrated in the central city.

The Logic of Urban Renewal As a Response

Urban renewal has, from the beginning, been a program aimed at *spaces*. Its key units—project and community—refer to the dispersion of sites and structures in space. This is because the logic of conventional real estate theory decrees that "no unit can rise above the ceiling set by its environment." Now, since 97 per cent of all housing in a given year consists of the "standing stock," the entire array of declining neighborhoods must be upgraded (or so runs the urban renewal argument). In the same vein, the economic health of the CBD is a function of its existing hinterland in space; to improve that health, residential hinterland must be upgraded. It all results in a fixation upon the given spatial pattern and the land use inherent in that pattern.

The key metaphor is derived from the map. What, then, is the appropriate spatial unit for analysis? One might sensibly say, the extent of urban settlement constituting a single matrix of housing markets, job markets, retail markets, industrial complexes, financial chains, and, in short, the metropolitan area as a whole. If one chose it he could then ask: What have growth and time done to the collective fortunes of those living and working here? What has happened to the total housing inventory, the total retail trade, the summed activity of business, finance, industry, education, welfare, and other crucial activities of urban life?

One would find, in general, "upgrading." Better housing for a larger proportion of the people, more and better universities, museums, shopping centers, and so on. True, some have declined in relative importance—the CBD has experienced a changed market in quality and to some degree in quantity—but this is inevitable. With dispersion, one expects subcenters; the "friction of space" gives advantages to the near at hand and the CBD is now only one among a number of giant subcenters.

It is also true that the areas of deteriorating housing are expanding in the old centers of the older cities. The slums are spreading, as the population of poor and residentially restricted Negroes increases. But this is just what one would expect if the poorly paid labor force is part of the growing economic complex. After all, the American population has grown by two-thirds in the past four decades, while our metropolitan population has increased by *over 130 per cent*. Everything has been expanding at a fierce rate in the metropolitan community, including the slums. Their failure to disappear only indicates that our efforts at slum elimination have not grown proportionately.

But the slums, *as a proportion of the metropolitan complex,* are not increasing—quite the reverse. They seem to be increasing only when we take them as a fraction of that minority of the metropolis located within the boundaries of the central city.

Those boundaries cut more than bold black lines on a map. As governmental boundaries between central city and suburbia they limit the distribution of activities on the face of the earth. For, since the effects of spatially defined renewal programs can only affect given *jurisdictions,* the metropolitan area is not the chosen unit. Instead, urban renewal is concentrated upon those governmentally defined units with enough problems and enough power to mark out (and try to stamp out) "slums" and "CBD blight." These are the central cities. Their fiscal problems are continuous, their mayors are looking for help, and their electorate *en masse* is a major part of the national vote.

Looking then at "the city" as if it were limited to the older, central, incorporated district, the figures change radically. From 15 to 40 per cent of the dwelling units are usually substandard (equals blight, equals slum.) The proportion of local retail trade in the CBD has declined proportionally and often there is even a decline in absolute dollars. Population is beginning to dwindle, and fewer people (but more cars) enter the downtown shopping district. There have been no new buildings built in downtown for ten (fifteen, twenty, twenty-five) years. It is a picture of gloom.

Yet this is the result to be expected. The changing space-time ratio has shifted the basic market values of central city sites; time has changed the value of structures. Greater freedom of choice and changing structures have changed use, thus land value, thus taxes. Much of the central city is not desirable for middle-class residence, for "quality" trade, or for new industrial plants because better alternatives are available to the locating organizations. Shussheim has put it succinctly:

Federal grants are made to individual localities, many of which are within larger metropolitan regions. Few localities receiving federal grants make systematic benefit-cost studies. Those that do will pursue their own self-interest. But what is best for the individual locality is not necessarily best for the region. There is no overall hand—visible or invisible—that attends to this.[13]

Urban renewal is an attempt to revive the city-state, at a time when the permeability of boundaries is the most striking aspect of spatial units. Ignoring the working relations between part and whole, the program is concentrated upon the part as an entity in itself and this partiality is both a weapon and a trap. It is a political weapon used in the market competition among subcenters in the metropolitan complex: Federal money spent to revive the CBD is subsidizing competition with the shopping centers of the outer city and the suburbs. It is a trap for those concerned with improving the gross supply of housing in the metropolis, since it ignores the positive benefits of suburban dispersion, an increased supply of "decent" housing for the ethnics forced to remain in the central city. The overall utility of this urban renewal strategy can be gauged more effectively by examining the tactics used in achieving each goal, slum elimination and CBD blight removal.

Tactics of Slum Elimination and Prevention

In Chapter 4 of this study, it was pointed out that the officials responsible for local urban renewal programs are by no means agreed upon the importance of housing goals. Some wish to divorce the program from them; others aspire to make "the first city without slums." Even among those committed to the latter view, there is a wide range of goals. At one extreme is the position of the housing official of the Jamaican government who says:

[13] Morton J. Shussheim, "Determining Priorities in Urban Renewal," *Papers and Proceedings of the Regional Science Association,* VI (1960), 204.

"I'm interested in housing—in putting people behind doors. That's all. What they do then is none of my business—I'm not a social worker and I don't know how to run their lives. There's too much of that."

At the other extreme are those who feel that the problems uncovered by urban renewal projects in the slums have tentacles extending into all parts of the society.

Some of the ambiguity of the slum elimination program stems from the use of the term "slum" as a sponge word. By the Jamaican official's criteria, a city of standard housing would be slum-free. By the terms of administrative definitions in America, this would also be true. (One code-enforcement official thought condemnation of standard neighborhoods would, in fact, be unconstitutional in his state.) A non-slum would, by these criteria, be any area of standard housing. Why are so few persons satisfied with this definition?

First, and of some importance, is the belief that "ways of life" must be changed if one is to ever abolish substandard neighborhoods. For, when new housing is impossible, rehabilitation is the only possibility and it can only be financed at present by the income, time and energy of the slum dweller. Then too, rehabilitated housing can only be maintained if the dweller is committed to maintenance. But in a broader sense, many advocates of slum elimination turn to nonhousing factors because they see slums as the logical result of *poverty*. The poor cannot afford standard housing. Therefore the poor will have to be made less poor—or housing will have to be subsidized. Such a position is held by those who remark that some families could not do a maintenance job if a house were given to them free. Ways of life are important to some, then, because they are seen as causes of substandard housing.

But another major reason for the rejection of slum elimination as simply a housing construction goal is the conceptual one. In truth, the old identification of a range of conditions seen as "problems" with *given spatial areas,* and the designation of the latter as "the slums," is still very much alive. (Cf. Chapter 2.) It is a designation that confuses housing as cause with housing as effect. Such confusion has political consequences; Dean argued that our housing programs have been established through the use of myths which "prove" that poor housing produces poverty, crime, and disease. The value of removing such neighborhoods is then "proved" by comparing the costs of the areas to the city in services, as against the taxes collected there.[14] The distinction between poor housing (as administratively defined) and these other social ills, however, has been made emphatically clear through the performance of slum residents transplanted to public housing projects. Jane Jacobs speaks of such projects as simply "immuring the slums."[15]

It is because those concerned with slum elimination care about the *social* attributes of poor neighborhoods that they resent a definition embracing only the quality of housing. Conceptual ambiguity is built into the present Housing Act through the undefined nature of the term "slum." The hiatus allows some to maintain that slums result from housing and building layout or from lack of building maintenance, while others see *their* slums as the results of social conditions, personality problems, or some combination of the two. This variation results from shifting definitions of the term; conceptual ambiguity results in operational confusion.

The Nature of Slums

Clarification of the concept must begin with a separation of housing conditions from other conditions of the slum population. Indeed, they have no one-to-one correlation; poverty, disease, and crime appear in many neighborhoods of standard housing. The poverty of the shabby genteel is as grinding as any other; communicable diseases frequently

[14] John P. Dean, "The Myths of Housing Reform," *American Sociological Review*, Vol. XIV, No. 2 (April 1949), pp. 281–288.
[15] Jacobs, *Death and Life*, 130 ff.

emanate from hospitals (as recent studies of staphylococcus epidemiology demonstrate); crime may be rampant in the North Shore suburb where teenagers are addicts of their medical father's cocaine. Conversely, as Gans has shown in his Boston study, rather poor housing can contain law-abiding, healthy, working-class populations. This is true in American cities; it is strikingly true when we change culture and climate and observe a city such as Kingston, Jamaica, where 80 per cent of *all* families live in one-room houses.[16]

There seem to be two broad classes of problems involved in the concept "slum." There are, first, *housing problems*—to get housing acceptable by administratively defined criteria financed, built, and occupied by the "problem" population. Secondly, there is a potpourri of *social problems*—to eliminate or prevent the deviation of some people's behavior from the norms of acceptable behavior. Such deviation includes crime, illness, and poverty (though some contend that, in America, poverty is automatic proof of crime).

The two kinds of problems do interact, empirically, in American cities. The allocation of housing by income means that the poor will be concentrated in given housing of lowest price; this is apt to be spatially concentrated because it is similar in age and type, and because the aggregate constitutes the environment for any given house. McKenzie put it this way:

> The slum is the area of minimum choice. It is the product of compulsion rather than design. The slum therefore, represents a homogeneous collection as far as economic competency is concerned, but a most heterogeneous aggregation in all other respects.[17]

This definition requires two important qualifications. First, when those who could go elsewhere do not choose to, the housing-finance correlation breaks down. Secondly, when choice is restricted on other than economic grounds, as in the case of racial restriction, the

[16] *The Economic Development of Jamaica*, International Bank for Reconstruction and Development (Baltimore: Johns Hopkins Press, 1952).

[17] R. D. McKenzie, "The scope of Human Ecology," Publications of the *American Sociological Society*, XX (1926) 141–154, reprinted in *Studies in Human Ecology*, ed. by George A. Theodorson (Evanston, Illinois: Row, Peterson and Company, 1961), p. 35.

"homogeneity" again breaks down. Thus McKenzie's statement is not, properly speaking, a definition: It is an empirical proposition concerning the interaction of housing and population attributes. Reformulated, it might run: "*If* housing is distributed strictly by ability to pay, the poorest will be aggregated in the cheapest housing; this is the area of minimum choice which some call slums."

More generally, concentrations of substandard housing are usually occupied by *those with the least social choice.* They are, relatively speaking, "losers" in the general population changes described earlier. Their range of choice is restricted by their social rank, their ethnic identification, or their life style—or by all three in combination. Each deserves a word of explication.

Those of lowest social rank, with little formal education and, consequently, undemanding and poorly paid jobs, have little to bid with in a competitive market. Replaceable parts of marginal importance to their employers, their income is intermittent: they are partly attracted to cheap neighborhoods by the possibility of paying the rent in weekly installments rather than in one monthly bill. Their lack of opportunity for upward mobility by job or income further cements their commitment to the cheapest housing available. They are indeed limited by their "minimum economic competency."

Those of ethnic status, segregated by the preferences of those who control the housing market, are in different case. McEntire and his associates have documented, extensively, the structure that limits the residential choices of Negroes, Puerto Ricans, Mexicans, and other physically defined populations. The findings leave no doubt that real estate brokers occupy a key position in the restrictive chain: Typical is the bylaw of a local real estate board in St. Louis.

No member of our board may, directly or indirectly, sell to Negroes or be a party to a sale to Negroes, or finance property for sale to or purchase by Negroes, in any block, unless there are three separate and distinct buildings in such block already occupied by Negroes.[18]

[18] Quoted in Davis McEntire, *Residence and Race,* Final and Comprehensive report to the Commission on Race and Housing (Berkeley and Los Angeles: University of California Press, 1960), p. 241.

This exclusionist tactic is reinforced by policies of financial institutions which, as in San Francisco, require "that the property securing the loan be within an established Negro neighborhood."[19] Since Negro neighborhoods are largely made up of older houses, the limitation to such neighborhoods is, in effect, limitation of one's right to purchase dwellings that will serve as security for a loan. Then too, until quite recently the federal government's own mortgage financing policy (based on the recommendations of Homer Hoyt and other experts in the field) accepted the proposition that Negro residents destroyed the real estate values of a neighborhood and the FHA counseled against loans. Finally, builders have been unable to build for Negroes on land of fair value for residences because of zoning laws and the way they are enforced in given municipalities. In short, the "free market" has been shot through with political combinations aimed at restricting ethnic housing choice. The result has been to provide a captive market for those who own property that can be sold or rented to ethnic minorities.

There are some residents of the substandard areas who are restricted to cheap housing because of their own norms. They may put other amenities before housing, or they may have no desire for home-ownership. Abu-Lughod and Foley show the sharp decline in the desire for home-ownership as income declines: Only half of their relief recipients wanted to own a home.[20] But the supply of cheap *rental* housing is much more restricted than that of owner-occupied housing; it tends to be in the central city, disproportionately concentrated in the "gray areas." This is where 80 per cent of the substandard supply of metropolitan areas is found. Finally, some choose the area because they cannot imagine leaving the relative safety of their working-class, ethnic neighborhood.

That neighborhood is frequently defined, by middle-class, non-ethnic observers, as simply "the ghetto." As we have noted earlier, however, it may be more important as a protective community and a valuable social world. Ryan, in summarizing his anthropological study of a Boston "slum" concludes:

19 *Ibid.*, p. 224.
20 Abu-Lughod and Foley, *Housing Choices and Constraint.*

Our analysis reveals that West End culture differs markedly in pattern and in emphasis from the nominal system sometimes referred to as the dominant—or, in the terminology of others, middle class—American pattern. Salience was invested in two critical areas: integration, the holding together of a markedly differentiated sociocultural system, as exemplified in the value of ethnic harmony; and expressiveness, an orientation to involvement in and enjoyment of human relationships in the present, as exemplified in the friendliness configuration. West End culture placed its highest valuation precisely in this latter area. In contrast, there was much less emphasis placed on instrumental striving. Thus, occupational goals tended to be modest, relatively immediate and subordinate in significance to human relational considerations.[21]

Similar working class cultures have been identified in East London, Syracuse, and other cities. The area called a slum by an outsider may be a major social value, the result of those "human capital investments" represented in kinship, friendship cliques, and a network of mutual aid and play relations. The quality of housing is more or less a historical accident, partly due to the difference in housing standards between the residents and outsiders. It would be interesting to see what housing codes the residents would devise.

The consequences of these three sets of limits is to define the characteristics of those typically resident in substandard housing concentrations. They are poor, segregated by color, or committed by an ethnic and/or working-class style of life to cheaper rental units in the central city. They are not necessarily criminals or other deviant types; they are not necessarily disease contracting or distributing. Yet there are interactions between those selectively channeled into the substandard housing supply and the latter conditions.

In approaching this relationship, it is useful to separate "charac-

[21] Ryan, "Individual Identity"; for the East London studies, see Michael Young and Peter Willmott, *Family and Kinship in East London* (New York: The Free Press, 1957); the Syracuse findings are based on personal communications with Seymour Bellin, Irwin Deutscher, and S. M. Miller of the Syracuse Youth Development Authority, Syracuse University. Other relevant studies include Hilda Jennings, *Societies in the Making* (London: Routledge and Kegan Paul, 1962), a study of working-class society in Bristol and Morris Janowitz, *The Community Press in an Urban Setting* (Glencoe: The Free Press, 1952), a study of three neighborhoods of Chicago.

teristics concepts" from "interaction concepts."[22] While the concentration of populations *may* be a result of simple interaction between population characteristics and the housing market (including political decisions ruling the latter) the population, once *in situ*, also interacts and produces a social environment. This social product seems to be what we usually mean by the slums. It is characterized by danger to person and property and by poor neighborhood housekeeping.

The maintenance of safety and order in a residential neighborhood is dependent upon the normative structure, the publicly accepted morality of the residents. This, in turn, derives from commitment to the neighborhood and a sufficient similarity in social characteristics to allow communication and agreement.[23] Upon these bases interdependence is translated into order: Sanctions may operate and the rules of the road be enforced. The neighborhood is a "quasi primary" structure, a result of commitment to home and household. As such it is capable of producing a minimal and conservative collective response to collective problems. It is not, however, either an agency for mass adult education or a command post for the radical solution of common problems.

Most of the populations that locate in areas of substandard housing are not promising material for such neighborhood order. Except for ethnic enclaves, such as the West End, their commitment is apt to be slight. (A majority would like to move.) Their heterogeneity by all criteria except rent is not conducive to common norms. Furthermore, the likelihood that many will be poorly educated and rural in origin means they have no past experience of appropriate rules of the road. In short, they are a captive population collected through a market that registers only their minimal choice.

To be sure, those who have a more than minimal choice and locate in the area because of kinship, class, and ethnic ties, would present a different case. However, their importance in the general result would

[22] I am indebted to the work of Herbert Gans for a radical clarification of this problem. See especially his forthcoming volume on Levittown.

[23] For an explication, see Scott Greer, "The Social Structure and Political Process of Suburbia" in *American Sociological Review*, Vol. XXV, No. 4 (August 1960), pp. 514–526.

vary with their proportion of the total population mix. Evidence indicates that, where a large majority share common ethnic background, family ties, and organizations such as the Catholic Church, there are some grounds for a normative order. (It is usually accompanied by homeownership.) But the Negro who hesitates to leave Harlem or the South Side is chiefly reacting negatively to the unknown "white man's world" out there. His own fellow ethnics share no distinctive cultural heritage excepting a rural origin and a common reaction to rejection by white society. Indeed, Negro areas become strong social neighborhoods only as class segregation allows the emergence of the middle-class, owner-occupied enclave. This leaves the poorest Negroes right where they were, in the unorganized neighborhoods of the tenements.

The lack of a strong moral order at the neighborhood level has many results. It allows problematic and unstable relationships among households, between adults and children, and among children. It produces a vacuum in control of the physical environment and the consequent litter of common scenes such as sidewalks, alleys, playgrounds, and yards. In forcing persons who do not know or trust each other to act within a common field, it increases objective danger and reinforces (by some very large multiplier) social distrust. Both danger and distrust are aggravated by the development of organized crime in the area (indigenous or immigrant) and the drift to cheap housing of the downwardly mobile and deviant—the narcotics and alcohol addicts, the ill, the senile, the sexually deviant, and so forth. No wonder the individual family turns inward. Irwin Deutscher tells of a visit in Syracuse to a resident in one shack of a row of dilapidated shacks.[24] Outwardly, it looked like all the others; inside it was completely renovated, shining in cleanliness and equipped with the latest consumer goods. The housewife had a simple explanation: The neighborhood was so dreadful that she refused to live in it. "I live in this *house*, not the neighborhood."

The weakness of the neighborhood as a normative structure has

[24] In personal communication.

further effects. It results in neglect by city officials charged with maintaining sanitation and safety of person and property, becoming to them chiefly a source of suspects, not a problem in policing. Residents are concerned about police protection, but it is chiefly protection *from* the police that they want. The difficulties of the police can be understood, whether or not with sympathy. Governmental agencies must depend upon surveillance and complaints by citizens and the citizens of such areas do not complain. Trash and garbage are not collected and the streets are not cleaned. (One wonders what the most prosperous of middle-class areas would look like if nobody ever came by to pick up their litter.) Officials tend to see these "slums" as a hostile country and, indeed, to control an area without the support of an indigenous social system is analogous to guerrilla warfare; it requires ten officers for each guerrilla.

Changing Slums by Urban Renewal

We can be very brief about it. Slums are produced by (1) the demand for low-quality housing among those with limited choice; (2) a supply of areally concentrated cheap housing, inadequate by current standards; (3) the social consequences of concentrating those with least choice as residents in a given area and; (4) the response to these social consequences by responsible agents of the society.[25] Each link in the chain is necessary; together they produce that social phenomenon which in common usage is called a slum.

To eliminate and prevent the further formation of such residential areas would seem in principle to be possible. Each of the four terms can be changed (though with very different consequences) to achieve

[25] This formulation owes a good deal to conversations with Anthony J. Downs and to his published and unpublished work. His emphasis, as an economist, is on points (1) and (2); as a sociologist I would underline (3) and (4).

the desired result. And all four could be changed simultaneously with another set of consequences. Any change, however, would exact a price. The *status quo* would be altered, scarce resources would be used, freedom of choice would shift, rights and duties would be changed; in short, values would be reallocated and some would win and some would lose.

But if this analysis is correct, the key variable is social choice. To eliminate slums, the range of housing choice for those who live in substandard areas must be extended in the direction of "standard" housing. This can be done by increasing the supply of standard housing that they can afford by lowering its price, raising their income, or both, if the limitations derive from income. If the limitations derive from their ethnic identity, which confines them to a segregated housing market, then the extension of that market is necessary. The effects of extension of choice would be, in general, a movement of the population from the locale where substandard housing is clustered. Such a solution is strictly based upon manipulation of the housing market: It does not depend on areal units. But choice can also be extended through rehabilitating the housing in a given area *en masse*. This would require that resources be put into the physical plant and the social structure of the neighborhood.

The housing consequences of either tactic should be clear: More of the population would end up in standard housing. But the social consequences would differ. In the first case, a widening range of accessible housing should result in the dispersion of the slum population among the nonslum population. They would move into neighborhoods where an existing order could "shape them up." (In the process one would, of course, destroy whatever values were a result of the existing social order, as in the case of Newark's North Ward and Boston's West End.) The acculturation of ex-slum dwellers would be particularly effective if they moved into areas of single-family dwelling units where homeowners constituted an organizational backbone for the neighborhood. Should they remain in the area of the slum, however, a massive adult education program would be required, combined with the education of city officials in charge of inspection and policing.[26]

The widening of objective choice, of alternatives, is not the same thing as increasing moral choice. The reorganizing of slum neighborhoods requires a change in normative order. It can come about only through persuasion, education, or force. The usual tactic has been the latter, where the moral problem is evaded through the decrease of alternatives. This is the implicit logic of slum clearance and code enforcement. If substandard housing is illegal, it can be condemned and razed, and housing choices will vanish in the process.

The two techniques were combined in the original slum clearance program, the Housing Act of 1937. For every substandard unit destroyed, a standard public housing unit was built. Thus in theory the total range of alternatives moved toward standard housing, public or private. The goal of the present urban renewal program is the same. In theory the ability to choose substandard housing shrinks, as the supply is destroyed by code enforcement and urban renewal projects, while neighborhood rehabilitation, public housing, relocation housing, and the private market are expected to produce replacement housing. Consumer choice in housing (which might lead a family to choose cheaper housing and a better automobile) is obviated through the destruction of the cheaper housing while, at the same time, more standard housing is made available.

But this is not the way the program works. The barriers to the increase in housing choice for slum populations have proved rigid and they are still based upon social rank, ethnicity, and life style. Increasing the housing supply for the very poor is not a profitable market operation; public housing, the alternative, is not a politically popular program. As Grigsby puts it, FHA is not for the poor. Even the better risks among the poor suffer from biases in FHA policy.

Cheaper homes and lower-income families did not meet government credit standards. The anomaly is that the government agencies with supposedly

[26] Cf. Millspaugh and Breckenfeld, *Human Side of Urban Renewal*, Chap. 1, 2, 3, for a discussion of the size of this task.

advanced underwriting concepts backed away from risks that private enterprise was willing to accept. . . . Those who achieved ownership despite the
bias in the government programs paid higher interest rates and in some
cases higher prices than they would have with FHA or VA financing.[27]

And the rehabilitation program may, in fact, decrease the supply of
low-cost housing:

> Preservation and restoration at one point may be achieved at the cost of
> an equivalent or greater reduction in the pace of improvement through new
> construction. Moreover, it must be remembered that it is upgrading by
> abandonment which provides most low-income families with homes.[28]

Thus urban renewal has the general effect of squeezing out the poorest from rehabilitation areas (through lack of investment cash, credit,
or rents) and preventing "filteration" through discouraging new
construction. Meanwhile total redevelopment produces a net deficit
in low-cost housing, and high-rent apartments which go up in place
of the central-city slum neighborhoods only compete with high-rent
apartments in the suburbs. Neither has a consequential effect upon
the supply of low-cost housing.

As for ethnic restrictions on housing choice, the effects of urban renewal have been the same. Although Negroes occupy only about
one-fourth of the substandard dwelling units in the nation, nearly 70
per cent of the dwelling units condemned for urban renewal projects
have been Negro residences. This is largely due to their central location and deteriorated conditions, but the effects are the same as they
would be if dehousing Negroes were the goal. There is little indication that urban renewal has had any intention or effect of increasing
the housing open to Negro occupancy, with the exception of public
housing and a few relocation housing projects. Most of the 97 per
cent of housing in the "standing stock" remains closed to Negroes,
while a portion of that which is available to them is being destroyed.

[27] *Housing Markets and Public Policy*, p. 220.
[28] *Ibid.*, p. 233.

Public housing is open to Negroes. It is, in fact, rapidly becoming all-Negro in many cities, but this has only problematic consequences for *social* slum elimination. The public housing project is the area of minimal choice with a vengeance; the social attributes of the residents are no different when they live in projects than they were in the slums, and the social consequences are similar. With public housing, however, the slum does cease to be a housing problem; its roots in other social conditions become very evident. Thus public housing programs are moving, however timidly, toward counseling, group work, organizational manipulation—in short, adult education. As such they are probably more effective (at least potentially) than the unorganized urban neighborhood.

Meanwhile urban renewal projects, as they are sited in areas that are desirable to the private real estate industry, sometimes raze neighborhoods that are far from being slums in any social sense. Their proffer of public housing as compensation leaves the Negro family with the choice of substandard housing elsewhere or residence in public housing. For higher-income Negro families the squeeze may be greater, for they cannot even qualify for public housing. Such urban renewal activity tends to decrease housing choice for Negroes and, as it does so, to perpetuate (if not to increase) the area of the slums.

Nor does the destruction of substandard neighborhoods have a marked effect upon the housing of those who freely choose the slums. Whether because they choose to allocate income otherwise, or because they choose to live near the ethnic concentration, such persons seem to retain their preferences. Since code enforcement is highly selective, large areas of substandard housing remain for them to inhabit. While urban renewal does so little to increase the residential dispersion of the Negro population, the vast Negro ghettos will remain for them to choose. The net result is, usually, removal from the urban renewal project area to the nearest substandard neighborhood.

In short, if urban renewal cannot increase the range of housing choice for the residents of areas designated as slums, the tactic of decreasing choice to that which is socially prescribed cannot work. At an extreme, the net product would be dehousing. But long before that extreme is reached, the system for decreasing choice breaks down. Code enforcement centers on the "easy areas," leaving the overutilized and undermaintained housing as it is. As these areas spread, the result is relocation of the slums.

One would expect resistance to Negro dehousing to increase as its import becomes widespread; as this occurs, the thrust behind urban renewal will have to be greater. Projects must pay off in a major way for powerful organizations in the city, for they will have a political price tag. Though residents of any given project area may be helpless, the organized opinion of Negro voters will be something to take into account.

The urban renewal program *for the slum dweller* is the program of rehabilitation. (Redevelopment seems actually to be a program aimed against him.) But rehabilitation does not increase the housing choices of the very poor; it further limits them. At the same time, the program is itself limited by the choices available to those with greatest freedom: Though they are the natural armature of the neighborhood organization, they are also most likely to leave voluntarily. (Nor can one argue that they should not: yet in the present program, as Grigsby says, "no recognition is given to the fact that some families would be better advised to invest in a home elsewhere.")[29] Neighborhood rehabilitation also suffers from the general fixation on spatial areas built into the urban renewal effort. It is true that neighborhoods represent social capital, but when that capital value is derived from a *politically* limited housing market (as in the case of Negroes and other segregated ethnics) rehabilitation amounts to a reinforcement of existing constraints on social choice.

Thus urban renewal does not decrease the demand for substandard housing. Insofar as it destroys the existing stock accessible to those with the least choice, it actually increases demand and price and therefore decreases the quality and quantity available at a given

[29] *Ibid.*, p. 243.

price. The code enforcement program is limited to what can be enforced and, as the low-income and Negro populations get less housing of poorer quality for their dollar, more housing falls below code standards: substandard housing is increased. The social consequences of concentrating those with less choice in one area are probably affected to a degree by rehabilitation, but at the price of dehousing those with truly minimal freedom.

The response to these social consequences by other responsible agencies of the society has not yet been discussed as a variable. However, it is another part of the "slum complex" that could be changed radically. One possibility is a substantial increase in the budget committed to rehousing and retraining the poor and to destroying the political barriers to housing that segregate colored citizens. Schoolteachers, policemen, inspection officers, public maintenance workers, and the like could be assigned in greater number to the slum areas. As the jobs are more difficult, they could be screened for higher abilities and paid premium salaries. The social characteristics of the population, the housing of the population and the neighborhood social structure of the population, would be the *foci* in a search for solutions to the various "problems" as defined.

Such changing definitions are in some evidence, but not in the urban renewal program. What appears to be occurring there is something quite different—the selective enforcement of standards. As the program is increasingly sponsored by mayors and CBD businessmen, it concentrates on improving the looks and value of selected central city areas. This is, to be sure, a kind of redefinition of the response of societal agents: Some would call it a Potemkin Village strategy, which defines the problem away.

Blight Removal and Urban Renewal

"The real surge nowadays is for the removal of CBD blight." Thus spoke the director of a program in one very large city and his proposition seems correct. If urban renewal is increasingly viewed as chiefly a tool to remove central-city blight, we must again ask: How do we know if a central city is such a problem? And, if so, where did the problem come from?

"Blight" is merely a poetic metaphor indicating the decline of use and value in areas which were once high on these particular scales. Chester Rapkin has carefully described a "blighted" area in New York City. In summary:

1. In the last twenty-one years, living space has been constant, but population has increased by over 50 per cent. It is over 40 per cent nonwhite.
2. There has been an increased turnover of property, a decline in duration of ownership, declining assessed value, rising costs, decreasing market prices.
3. There has been an increasing proportion of second mortgages, little new money is available, interest rates are high, repayment periods are short (five to ten years), and premiums of 10 to 30 per cent are required on the loans above interest.
4. There is a high ratio of rents to equity; gross rent multipliers are very low, with little variation by quality of building, averaging around four or five. That is, the building's value is only a few times a gross annual rent.[30]

In short, the property no longer has the values it once had. Once resident here were the stable-to-prosperous middle-class; in the New York of 1910–1920, these brownstones were symbols of achievement. These shops were quality shops and specialty shops. Today it is an area of working-class people, one-third Puerto Rican, living in crowded quarters and shopping at little corner stores.

The story is common in the central areas of American cities. The older symbols of the top now stand for the bottom in value. The center of downtown has moved away; the wealthy and prosperous live in the suburbs; the "100 per cent corner" of yesterday is the skid row of today. These changes, however, have been spotty and irregular; some

[30] *The Real Estate Market in an Urban Renewal Area* (New York: New York City Planning Commission, 1959), pp. 85 ff.

corners are still flourishing, and some areas of the CBD are still high in value. Some people still have a major commitment to the down-town. Seeing in the vacant and underused structures the symbolized importance of the area in the past, some are committed to reconstituting it in the present.

But values flow from use. So as use of the CBD declines among many kinds of people, commitment to the area as "hallowed ground" also begins to decline. Of how many cities can one say, as Kevin Lynch does of Los Angeles:

> The central area is still by courtesy "downtown," but there are several other basic cores to which people are oriented. The central area has intensive shopping but it is no longer the best shopping, and great numbers of citizens never enter the downtown area from one year to the next.[31]

While commitment is weakening, reconstitution is becoming more costly. For the "multiplier" effect, which leads to a great advantage when facilities are massed, begins to work in reverse as they are separated; one gets a "divider" effect. As the firms with branches in both downtown and the suburban shopping centers close their downtown shop, the net value of the downtown district to the user rapidly shrinks. The size of the reconstitutive effort must increase.

Title I Redevelopment is based upon the assumption that cleared land for new starts in the CBD will lure enterprises to the location. The cost of acquiring the land and demolishing the structures is high in terms of public moneys expended, and there are other costs. There is also, as we have noted, a cost to those displaced: If they had few alternatives in the first place (as in the case of the Puerto Rican slum dwellers) it may be very high. There is also the cost to other sub-centers within the metropolitan area—the lost business and lost taxes in the suburbs. And, insofar as the projects succeed, the commutation of suburban residents to the CBD is a net cost in transportation.

Yet the total costs are hardly reflected in the increased advantages

---

[31] *The Image of the City* (Cambridge: Technology Press and Harvard University Press, 1960), pp. 32–33.

of those enterprises returning to the CBD. Land cost is a small fraction of total operating overhead, whether for business, industry, offices, or apartment houses. Those enterprises with existing investments in the CBD, land, structure, businesses, certainly have an interest in remaining and in improving their values. But new locatees have a wide range of choice; even if land is sold to them at less than value, the advantage is small. By law, however, it must be sold at a "fair market value." Thus new construction does not gain but the public loses, for the cost of Title I derives from the fact that land was purchased and readied for sale at a cost *above* market value.

The key question is this: How many enterprises will locate in the CBD that would not have done so anyway and at what cost? Unless there is a net increase in the use of the CBD, new building is wasted: One is, in effect, pouring water from one jar into another. The new office buildings in the urban renewal area may be filled with tenants at the cost of raising the vacancy rate in the rest of downtown to a level where it is all defined as "blight." Further, the use of public money pegs the market for land: The speculative increase in prices then discourages conversion to new uses, required if there is an oversupply of offices. An economist has put it this way:

> It was assumed that the principal obstacles to replacement of deteriorated property were on the cost and supply side. Developers would line up for central parcels of land if they could get them in the right size and at the right price. Little attention was paid to the market demand for such sites. The demand was presumably there but repressed.
>
> These assumptions may have been valid for a medieval city confined within a massive moat. . . . But they bore little relation to the technological facts of life in the 1950's.[32]

Few careful demand studies have been made before urban renewal project sites were cleared. One suspects fewer sites would be cleared if more were made.

Lyman Brownfield, General Council for the Housing and Home

[32] Morton J. Shussheim, "Urban Renewal and Local Economic Development," paper given before the New York Chapter, American Institute of Planners, December 9, 1960.

Finance Agency in 1960, has expressed concern about the possibility of absorbing the cleared land in the real estate market.

> Congress has made available through June 30, 1961, $2 billion of capital grant funds for urban renewal projects. . . . Since much of this urban real estate is located in high-density areas, the value of construction in relation to the value of the property is fairly high, so that the resulting values from the urban renewal projects for which capital funds have already been authorized may reasonably be expected to total $15 billion to $25 billion. And, of course, nobody expects the program to stop here. . . . Yet, in order to maintain a pace of disposition which I believe is necessery, which seems reasonable to me, and which may even seem modest to some, *we shall have to sell twice as much project land during each of the next ten years as has been sold in the entire preceding ten years.* [Italics mine.] [33]

Yet the organizations most concerned with urban renewal, the American Municipal Association, the National Association of Housing and Redevelopment Officials, and the United States Conference of Mayors, present estimates of urban renewal needs to the government "without giving any consideration to disposition progress as a limiting factor." [34] Commitment to the hallowed ground, the CBD, could hardly go further.

It seems likely that some new building is feasible in the CBD of most cities. There are, after all, functions of centrality; there are enterprises that find central location very much to their advantage. Raymond Vernon has assayed the future of New York City from this perspective. He sees a bright future for the very center, the clustering towers of mid-Manhattan. Nevertheless, in his words, the New York Metropolitan Region Study's projections

> . . . cast doubt on any image of the Region as a giant cluster of human activity held together by a great nub of jobs at the center. Instead, apart from the special problem offered by New York City's projected increase of half a million jobs or so, it affords a picture of a Region in which the centripetal pull is weakening. [35]

[33] Brownfield, "The Disposition Problem in Urban Renewal," *Law and Contemporary Problems,* Vol. XXV, No. 4 (Autumn 1960), p. 737.

[34] *Ibid.,* p. 735.

[35] *Metropolis 1985,* p. 224.

One of the major limits on CBD development is its market in retail trade. Since this is a direct product of its residential hinterland, one suspects that some of the regrets voiced because urban renewal projects cannot house the displaced poor are crocodile tears. Urban renewal planners hope to entice the middle-class back to the central city. Rapkin and Grigsby have made a careful analysis of the probable market for middle-income apartment housing in downtown Philadelphia and, in a metropolitan complex of around four million persons, they can see a demand for no more than eight thousand new dwelling units over a twelve-year period. The kind of people who choose such units are, with startling uniformity, prosperous couples without children, employed in the central city.

> It has frequently been asserted that larger families have avoided center city primarily because suitable accommodations are not available. . . . The recent marketing experience of several new apartment houses has shown us that even when substantial numbers of large units were made available they rented very slowly. . . .
>
> It thus appears that center city will be limited to the type of family currently resident in the area, and it is primarily for this reason that the demand for housing accommodations will rise but modestly by 1970. This increase will be sufficient to absorb a major portion of the land available for residential re-use in center city itself, but will not be great enough to support a renewal program in the massive sections of slum and deterioration that lie beyond the central core.[36]

The social choice that allows a familistic way of life also leads people to prefer the horizontal neighborhoods of suburbia. Vernon's conclusions are identical.

> As one surveys the outward shift of the populations in the New York Metropolitan Region and of the consumer activities tied to them, the forces behind the shift seem near-inexorable. Basic technological developments in transportation and deep-seated changes in consumer wants appear to lie behind the phenomenon. Here and there one sees evidence of preferences which breast the main tide; the occasional reappearance of a disillusioned

[36] Chester Rapkin and William G. Grigsby, *Residential Renewal at the Urban Core* (Philadelphia: University of Pennsylvania Press, 1960), pp. 116 ff.

exurbanite in his former city haunts, the gradual growth of apartments-in-the-city for the very rich—these are phenomena whose impact cannot be overlooked. The bigger risk, however, is that their implications for the future will be exaggerated rather than overlooked. Short of some fundamental alteration in consumer outlook or in urban environment, the trends for the future seem likely to represent a continuation—even a speed-up—of the dispersive tendencies of the past.[37]

This analysis agrees in all particulars with that of Abu-Lughod and Foley. They note that, "The suburban dream prevails among most consumers in whatever location [within the metropolitan area] and whatever section of the country. The suburban urge is strongest among young families with children living in large cities. . . ."[38] These are, of course, the major source of new housing commitments and, as they go on to conclude, "The family with children, seeking an owned home, represents the major force in the expansion of the suburbs." [39] If such families are to be lured back into the central city, massive changes will be necessary in the urban renewal program, for they want horizontal homes, not high-rise apartments at $45 per room. (There are at present strong indications that Manhattan is overbuilt with such housing. Those signing new leases are rewarded with free rent, a trip to Miami, and other fringe benefits for cooperating with the move to lure them back to the city.)

For such reasons, the removal of blight is apt to be rigidly limited to the center of the CBD. Home-offices, banks, insurance companies, communication firms, and the like, have a need for central location. The prosperous childless who work in such concerns will rent apartments in the area. Yet it will be a small island in the sea of working-class people and older buildings making up the central city. "Just beyond, for miles in every direction, we are likely to see a continued thinning out and aging of populations. . . ."[40]

The blight removal program proceeds under the assumption that CBD blight is, somehow, a net social loss. It is difficult to see why

[37] Vernon, *Metropolis,* p. 165.
[38] Abu-Lughod and Foley, *Housing Choices,* p. 187.
[39] *Ibid.,* p. 131.
[40] Vernon, *Metropolis,* p. 160.

this is so. The relative decline of the downtown districts merely reflects the changing space-time ratio and the changing advantage of centrality. Though income is lost to the proprietors of the CBD, it is regained by their competitors in the suburbs; though taxes are lost to the central city government, they are collected by the suburban municipality. Looking at the metropolitan area as a whole, blight that results from a change in location within the area is no loss. The program of blight removal is, then, a very cumbersome method of redistributing income from other subcenters to the old central business district, from suburbs to central city. It is possible to bring it off, within limits, but at what opportunity costs?

The older areas of the city are not necessarily devoid of value. The crowded quarters of Negroes, Puerto Ricans, and those non-ethnics who are merely poor, indicate the utility of these spaces for them. Thus the cost of forced change, through redevelopment or rehabilitation, is born by those with the fewest alternatives, those who are already paying a higher rent (in terms of marginal utility) than the rest of the population. These central-city slum dwellers, then, pay for the prospect of luring those with the greatest freedom of choice back from the suburbs. They pay when they are dehoused or when their landlords pass on the prices of improvement to them and prosper with increasing scarcity of competition.

Ironically, it is the inefficiency of the program that protects them. Title I, in general, causes urban renewal authorities to pay very high prices for slums. Thus the number that can be bought and destroyed is limited, leaving quarters for those with minimal housing choices. Of course this condition also increases greatly the cost of business properties and middle-class apartments, but this cost is born, not by real estate speculators, but by the federal government. And, since the government's funds come from an income tax disproportionately collected from the residents of suburbia, one might say that the suburban municipalities and shopping centers join the working-class ethnics of the central city in subsidizing a program to recreate the nineteenth century city of vague memory—the hub and center of the vanished metropolis.

Summary: Urban Renewal and the Social Environment

The discussion may be schematized. One can postulate three separate value-maps of the complex and interlinking sites for human action called an urban complex. Each map indicates the value of specific scenes, relative to others, for given purposes and by given measures. They are maps of locational use value, of inherited structures, and of the market's evaluations.

The map of locational use-value is based upon the requirements of the individual enterprises and households that are sited within the urban complex. This map has changed radically. Transport technology has altered the limits, increasing the geographical spread of sites which can continue to be integrated in common systems of action: The homes of workers can be located farther from the plant, the plant can be located farther from the market or the source of supplies. Other technological changes have modified the requirements of the plant: The use of continuous work-flows, based on moving belts, forklifts, and truck transport, requires large, horizontal areas and penalizes multi-story structures. Within the firm, the division of labor separates the routine processes from the innovation and negotiation of specialists; the latter may require a central location, the former may well be located in the suburbs. This is practical when instantaneous communication and contemporary transportation allow the two sets of behavior to be closely integrated.

The map of use-value for households is based upon the demands of the household, within the limits of what can be had. The demands of most American households today are, clearly, for the horizontal house on its own lot. These demands can be realized because of the increasing geographical space integrated in the metropolitan system, because of the rising income level, and because of the financial innovations that allow lifetime mortgages.

The map of structures, however, traces out the heritage of the nineteenth-century city. Appropriate to the use-values of an earlier technological epoch, it shows a dense concentration of high-rise commercial, industrial, and residential structures in the central city. Streets are appropriate to a world where most persons get about by public transport; there is no provision for parking adequate to the indigenous population, much less for visitors from other parts of the metropolis. Yet the patina of time lies on many of these older structures; they have a pious value for many.

But they do not have enough value to compete in the free market with newer structures, provided for newer uses and built to take advantage of the technological revolutions. And the map of market values within the metropolitan area shows clearly the competitive disadvantage of the nineteenth-century city. It loses out, not just because it is old, but because it is obsolete. It falls into disrepair because it is to nobody's advantage to maintain and use it in the fashion to which it was once accustomed. As Grigsby puts it, "With a few notable examples, the residential real estate market works only once. . . . The invisible hand, which only infrequently produces the optimum spatial deployment of land uses, with respect to renewal, typically produces nothing at all."[41] Thus the areas appropriate to investment yesterday are abandoned today. The reason is simple; there is more supply than demand for urbanized land.

The urban renewal program for reviving the central cities is based upon the assumption that market values will follow the map of *inherited structures,* bringing about a change in the use-value map of the metropolitan area. This is the logic behind the great investment in areas once highly valued in the pattern of activity making up the social city. But every principle of land use, of real estate dealership, and of common sense is violated by this assumption. *Structure is made obsolete by change in use-value* and not the opposite. The true sequence is one wherein the market-value follows the use-value of a site, modified somewhat but not reversed by the existing structure. The old building maintains some value because it has attributes that compen-

---

[41] *Housing Markets and Public Policy,* p. 251.

sate for the loss in locational advantages: It may be a Taj Mahal or, in American cities, may be usable for a Negro tenement.

Nor does urban renewal really swim against the current. Its continued acquiescence is guaranteed by its dependence upon the private real estate industry for new construction; its inability to subsidize allows private decisions to be made in terms of market estimates. In this respect it is, of course, no different from the FHA program or the federal highway program. Robert Wood, summarizing his study of the governmental impact on the development of the New York Metropolitan Region, says:

> The public programs expanding most rapidly in the Region are those that exhibit an operating philosophy most closely akin to a market economy. . . . In their political philosophy they are Manchesterian liberals, defining their public in terms of the individual buyer and striving to give the buyer what he wants. . . . The final result is that a public sector committed to this ideology by financing and structure offers no countervailing influence against the trends generated in the private sector. . . . They underwrite and accelerate the process of scatteration.[42]

[42] *1400 Governments*, pp. 171-172.

Chapter 7

URBAN RENEWAL AND THE FUTURE: WHAT CAN BE DONE?

Much of the confusion and downright contradiction in the present urban renewal program result from the unsystematic mixture of three quite different goals. The older goal of increasing low-cost housing, of eliminating and preventing slums, is mixed with the newer goal of revitalizing the central city; to both has been added the more recent goal of creating the planned American city through the community renewal program. But as these goals are translated into the actions of municipal bodies, based on local interests, they seem to be moving rapidly toward a program concerned only with revitalizing the central business district.

Such an outcome is possible when new goals are added, indiscriminately, to the tasks of existing programs. They roll up into one snowball of directives that allows no clear hierarchy of intentions and, therefore, no priorities. In evaluating the present program and suggesting how it might be made more effective, it is useful to discuss each goal separately, noting the interaction between the different efforts.

The Goal of Decent Housing

The urban renewal program has done little to increase low-cost housing. In fact, the policy of destroying occupied houses without providing any compensating new housing, has had the effect of decreasing the supply of low-cost housing. Yet American housing has improved strikingly since 1950. As Grigsby puts it:

> By the end of 1956 when occupied substandard housing had already dropped by more than 4,500,000 units, only one Title I project had been finished. . . . The principal cause seems to have been what is usually described in negative terms as the flight to the suburbs. This outward movement permitted lower-income families to vacate slum areas and acquire somewhat better quarters within the city.[1]

Thus the very trends that the central city redivivists deplore, the suburban "sprawl" and the growing areas of Negro and working-class neighborhoods in the old central city, were key factors in the improved opportunity of American families to achieve a "decent home."

What occurred was, simply, an expansion in the range of housing choice for those who lived in slums. This came about primarily through the increased supply of vacancies in the central city, close in space and price to the housing of the poor. The directive for improving housing would, then, seem clear: increase the supply of vacancies in such housing. Grigsby emphasizes two levers: changes in the credit available to low-income families and changes in marketing practices among real estate dealers. Though the very poor will generally rent discarded houses, those in the next higher income steps could afford new quarters competitive with their present homes. Thus, as the poor move from substandard to better houses, competition among land-

---

[1] In *Housing Markets and Public Policy*, pp. 261, 264. See also Beverly Duncan and Philip M. Hauser, *Housing a Metropolis—Chicago*, esp. Chap. 1 and 2, for a careful study of the same changes in one metropolis.

lords will produce a greater range of choice and a generally higher quality of housing.

Charles Haar, in his intensive study of the nature and impact of federal mortgage insurance programs, concludes:

> Government intervention through FHA and VA represents a facilitation subsidy and must be clearly recognized as such. The tendency to see in FHA a piece of private enterprise . . . produces a resistance to special programs—for the elderly, minority, or low-income groups—on the ground that these "social welfare" schemes distort the free-market pattern of operations, but . . . the part played by the Federal programs represents a subsidy to the housing industry. Although in time of depression it may be a sufficient justification to persuade lenders to lend and builders to build, in the long run this intervention is warranted only if it benefits the consumer . . .[2]

If Grigsby's analysis is correct, and I believe it to be, then the present FHA program must be extended toward lower-income groups. The assumption is not that the slum dweller can buy a new house, but that those who can do so will vacate quarters and thus yield him a wider range of choice. (In this respect, the forty-year mortgage program should be useful if it is sold to those who can afford it.)

In the light of the improvement in housing between 1950 and 1956, the reader may wonder why any new program is required. The reason is simple: "From 1950 to 1956 the oldest, cheapest, and presumably worst sections of the housing inventory appreciated more than did the higher quality units."[3] According to Grigsby's research, this is because the housing market is dichotomized by price; houses do not move easily from the middle- to lower-priced markets. In a key passage, Grigsby spells it out:

> A relatively small reduction of prices or rent in this range [i.e., the lower half of the market] should be very effective . . . in drawing families into the new construction market, [and] the dwelling units which they vacate are not

---

[2] Charles M. Haar, *Federal Credit and Private Housing,* The Mass Financing Dilemma (New York: McGraw-Hill Book Co., 1960), pp. 182, 188.

[3] Grigsby, *Housing Markets,* p. 186.

competitive with new single-family construction. . . . By contrast, stimulating the owner of say a $15,000 structure to purchase a new home in the
higher-price range leaves behind a dwelling unit that is competitive with another sector of the new construction market.[4]

Any program for improving housing must emphasize public housing, for there will remain households that cannot afford standard
housing. While they are around, they provide a captive market for
the worst structures in the city, thus giving a market value to the
slums. The political resistance to public housing has been discussed
elsewhere; sufficient to note, once more, the basic importance of the
program for any over-all effort at "rebuilding the cities." (As Grigsby
remarks, the 200,000 new units of public housing built between
1950–1956 may have been more important in reducing substandard
housing than all of the urban renewal programs put together.) Some
imaginative efforts are underway to improve the entire public housing scheme: the use of scattered second-hand housing, rent subsidy,
rental-purchase agreements, all appear to be promising new starts.
The emphasis upon housing for the aged seems likely to build, rather
rapidly, a cohort of grass-roots supporters. The population over sixty-
five is probably the largest single minority in the country today, with
low incomes, low education, and poor employment opportunities.
They are growing rapidly and, organized, may amount to a tangible
political force.

The second major limitation on housing choice is ethnic identity—
race. Today the increasing proportion of Negroes in central cities is
reflected in the spread of the Negro ghetto. This is another result of
the new starts in suburbia: As children of the central-city families
move to the tract developments and the old people die off, the houses
change hands and move into the segregated housing market.[5] This is

---

[4] *Ibid.,* pp. 205–206.

[5] There is every likelihood that this will occur in "Back of the Yards"; Millspaugh and
Breckenfeld note that the younger people are leaving despite a strong community organization and an all-out rehabilitation effort (*Human Side of Urban Renewal,* p. 216). Father
Berendt remarked, "If the young people will come back, the future looks good." Asked
if many are returning, he replied, "No, but some."

a logical flow; those with more choice opt for the new houses of suburbia; those with less choice find it expanded by central-city vacancies.

This process, however, has often been extremely destructive of social values. Negroes move slowly, saturating block after block; prices are inflated, space overutilized and undermaintained; the neighborhoods deteriorate. This is a result of containment. Negroes remain confined in the multiple-family dwelling units of the city, the proto-tenements, even though many younger couples would prefer and could afford to own single-family houses. Thus the segregated areas of the city expand but cannot change much in quality, for the same underlying conditions are present.

If Negro "invasion" of residential neighborhoods is not to produce "blight," a change in the rate of movement is necessary. Negroes must be able to distribute themselves in neighborhoods by their social rank and their style of life—their ability to pay and their household requirements. Luigi Laurenti has recently demonstrated the remarkable stability of housing values in racially mixed neighborhoods of single-family dwelling units where Negroes owned their homes. The commitment to the dwelling and the neighborhood affected Negroes in the same way it affects whites: Their input of energy, time, and money increased. In his analysis of Laurenti's findings, Anthony Downs emphasizes Negroes' ability to "leapfrog" over the dense neighborhoods of apartment houses to the horizontal neighborhoods of homeowners.[6] This, in turn, he traces to the softening "white housing" market and the movement of units into the tighter "Negro housing" market.

The proper policy for preventing blight would seem to be one of hastening the speed with which a wide range of housing units enter the Negro housing market. With rapidity of change and width of choice, the more familistic Negro households could concentrate in neighborhoods of single-family dwellings, could organize the main-

---

[6] Luigi Laurenti, *Property Values and Race* (Berkeley: University of California Press, 1960); Anthony Downs, "An Economic Analysis of *Property Values and Race*," *Land Economics,* Vol. XXXVI, No. 2, pp. 181–188.

tenance norms of those neighborhoods, and thus protect their investment. This would be possible only when poorer Negroes (or those
who do not opt for such areas) could find other housing, thus avoiding conversion of single-family areas into tenement clusters. Such a
policy would protect the social capital represented by the neighborhood as an environment—a major aim of urban renewal. It would
encourage the dispersion, therefore discouraging overcrowding and
substandard housing. It would allow a stable neighborhood framework within which unit maintenance and even the replacement of
units could be effected without requiring a massive adult education
program and the organizing of a political community.

There are many civic patriots who will shudder at such a possibility. For them a policy of "open occupancy" and the dispersion of
Negroes throughout the central city means a hastening of the day
when the city will be "run by the Negroes." It is well to keep some
figures in mind. The Commission on Race and Housing estimates
that the Negro population of northern and western cities will have
tripled at the end of the twenty-five-year period from 1950 to 1975;
this will be almost entirely a metropolitan—and a central city—
increase.[7] It is not a question of whether we shall have more Negroes
in our city. American laws allow free movement of labor, and
American industry continues to hire Negroes. The jobs are in the
metropolis and the available housing is in the central city.

The more important question is this: As Negroes become a major
part of the electorate, the political party, the government and clients
of government, how long shall they be treated as second-class
citizens? And, as they become first-class in terms of political power,
what kinds of interests and norms will they bring to the politics
of the central city? If it is true that men learn by doing and become
responsible through having power and responsibility delegated to
them, then the more rapidly Negro citizens gain parity of housing
rights the better. This includes the same rights to concentrate, by social rank and life style, as the whites do; the same right to organize

[7] McEntire, *Residence and Race,* pp. 20 ff.

by social class and exclude the poor and ignorant from your neighborhood. Such exclusive neighborhoods are, after all, the incubators of that middle-class style in politics so valued by American civic patriots.[8]

Even with open occupancy it is unlikely that many new central-city areas would become overwhelmingly Negro. Rentals would not decline and since the average Negro income is still substantially lower than that of whites, segregation by income would drastically limit the spread of mixed neighborhoods for years to come. Nor will the process of accommodation to the Negro in-migrant and the counter processes of educating him to city life be as interminable as they may look today. The farm labor force of the country has shrunk so rapidly that it is not much larger than the number of the unemployed; we are going to run out of rural migrants. Indeed, in the next few decades Negroes will become preponderantly urban born and raised. If this is correct, the nature of their urban environment is crucial. Neighborhoods, schools, political and occupational opportunities will all determine the outcome: They are all intertwined. But the neighborhood, representing the social environment and the spatial unit for the administration of public services, is a major variable.

Nor is the possibility of open occupancy, of homogenizing the housing market in the central city, as slim as it may seem. McEntire notes that a majority of northern and western citizens now indicate they would be willing to live in a mixed neighborhood.[9] As usual, the conventions of real estate dealers, financial institutions, and the government are far behind the reality. Nor is any deep commitment to racial equality required to bring a homogenized market about; indifference is much more dependable, or even resistance *overbalanced by the value of the housing.*

[8] For a discussion of the "ethnic" and "non-ethnic" styles in civic politics, and of the transition from the first to the second, see Edward C. Banfield and James Q. Wilson, *City Politics* (Cambridge: Harvard University Press and The M.I.T. Press, 1963), esp. Part III.

[9] *Residence and Race,* p. 79. Even in the South, 38 per cent said they would live in a mixed neighborhood.

As to racial attitudes, the fact that this group of home purchasers decided to buy in mixed areas implies that they were at least comparatively receptive to the presence of Negroes. However, in interviews, they did not express attitudes of unusual tolerance. If any were motivated by a desire to give a personal example of racial democracy they were few in number. More than a third of those interviewed expressed varying degrees of dissatisfaction with the presence of Negroes, but strongly negative sentiments were rare.[10]

In this connection, again, *rapidity* of change is desirable. If a widening range of housing is made available, Negroes are not apt to outbid each other to enter the same block. And this has important consequences for occupancy by whites. Rapkin and Grigsby discuss the mixed neighborhood in Philadelphia:

> The critical racial factors limiting the number of both prejudiced and unprejudiced white buyers who will purchase in mixed areas are the actual or expected number and proportion of nonwhites in the mixed community, and the spatial distribution of nonwhite residences in relation to the home which white buyers contemplate acquiring. . . . An increasing proportion of Negroes in a mixed area is reflected in a shrinkage in white demand. . . . In the past, it has been the most common expectation that a neighborhood once entered by nonwhites would become wholly occupied by them, and in most cases events have justified this anticipation. The present outlook however, is for an increasing number of neighborhoods where this expectation cannot be fulfilled.[11]

The results Rapkin and Grigsby discuss would be due to the increase of housing open to Negroes, beyond the effective demand for that housing. It seems likely that such an increase in choice, brought about by rapidly opening new neighborhoods to Negro buyers and renters, would result in a great social gain for the cities.

Negroes who move into higher quality housing leave those who remain in the slums a wider choice. They, in turn, can begin to vacate

---

[10] Chester Rapkin and William G. Grigsby, *The Demand for Housing in Racially Mixed Areas,* quoted in McEntire, *Residence and Race,* pp. 168–169. For similar findings, see Raymond W. Mack's study of the Lake Meadows project in Chicago (forthcoming).

[11] *Ibid.,* p. 171.

the worst slum quarters. As vacancy rates increase, the price of slum properties should rapidly sink, allowing them to be razed for code violations or condemned through eminent domain for redevelopment —and at a price far below what must be paid, in political backfires and cash, when scarce and occupied housing is destroyed by the civic authorities. The housing goal is endangered by destruction without replacement, but the achievement of the housing goal greatly facilitates destruction and redevelopment for other purposes. In Grigsby's words: "Demolition, as a general rule, should be the logical consequence of improvement in housing rather than the means of attaining it."

To be sure, there are indications that poorer Negroes spend a lower proportion of their income on housing than do whites.[12] This may indicate a lack of concern with housing; it may also indicate that the difference in quality bought for the few additional dollars they could afford (representing, however, a large proportion of their income) is negligible. Before we can tell, it is necessary that their money buy at least as much as that of whites. Increasing the housing choice of low-income and segregated populations should provide a test. With greater freedom to buy decent homes one would expect an increasing proportion of the Negro population to become homeowners. Should this occur, it is very likely that their proportionate investment in housing will rise sharply: Those who are committed to homeownership pay, in general, substantially more for the privilege than those who rent. Homeownership is part and parcel of the familistic life style that is increasingly popular with all Americans; with the opportunity to do so, Negroes will probably commit themselves to the same housing investment whites have made.

There remain those who are very poor, the aged, or the unemployed. These conditions are produced by machinery larger in scale than anything the city can control. They are beyond local solutions. The declining demand for unskilled labor when combined with

---

[12] Grigsby, *Housing Markets*, p. 286. See also C. F. Winnick, *Housing Choices and Constraints*, Part I, for a discussion of proportion of income spent in housing.

the inadequate training of the young produces a population of the permanently indigent, not only in the cities but in the small towns and open-country neighborhoods as well. At the same time, the increasing life-span results in a growing population of the poorly educated, poorly rewarded, poorly regarded, old. As *housing problems,* there is only one answer to their fate—publicly subsidized housing. A much more complicated answer is required for the gamut of problems they share.

The Goal of Revitalizing the Central City

The most spectacular new growth in central cities is the rise of headquarters buildings and high-rent, high-rise apartment houses. The skylines of New York and Chicago are in process of refurbishing at the moment. The growth is in the very center of the center, the CBD.

> Indeed, the most impressive renewal program of all has occurred in such a district without writedown of land costs, without use of eminent domain, without any other important public bounties. I have reference, of course, to the reconstruction in the postwar period of the East Side of Manhattan with office buildings and luxury housing. More than a billion dollars worth of private construction has been poured into this area since 1947.[13]

In Los Angeles dispersion means that the center is not a dot but a line, a measure of central tendency. Yet the development and redevelopment along Wilshire Boulevard, from the city center to the sea, is as impressive as the Third Avenue surge. Nor was urban renewal responsible: Growth of enterprises and jobs and the consequent demand for office space and housing were the dynamics.

When such demand for new space occurs, urban redevelopment seems to come about without public support. Without demand, it is not possible anyway. Shussheim continues:

[13] Shussheim, "Urban Renewal and Local Economic Development," p. 4.

But the warning flags are up: Vernon, Weimer and others have cautioned us that only a few regional centers can realistically hope for a heavy sustaining demand for new office space in their core districts.[14]

What then is the logic of urban renewal programs for revitalizing the central city? It is based upon the fact that land use may be frozen by multiple ownership and obsolete planning, which break land into too many fragments, each too small for contemporary demand. Land-use patterns are dependent upon the legal rights to use that land, and these are rigid indeed. (Grebler accounts for much of the persistence of land-use patterns in the rebuilding of bombed European cities through rigidities resulting from the existing patterns of ownership.)[15] Since redevelopment requires the assembly of many plots, the private redeveloper is at the mercy of the "holdout." The logic of the urban renewal program is, simply, to facilitate the aggregation of land so that new and more profitable uses are possible.

And indeed, such new uses may very well result if the land has intrinsic value as a site. The Diamond Heights development in San Francisco is apt to make a large profit for the local public authority, while scattered projects in other cities are net gainers. If, however, the potential market value really exists, the land should *always* make a profit. If it does not, use is being deflected from other parts of the urban complex at a net social cost. In other words, if commercial and industrial redevelopment are sensible, they should not ordinarily require subsidy.

Instead, the power of eminent domain and the right to borrow funds for the temporary acquisition of land should be adequate. Since the benefits and interests are strictly local, these powers should be granted to the local development agency by the state, along with the responsibility for their use. With scarce funds and a broad assign-

---

[14] *Ibid.*, p. 4.

[15] Leo Grebler, "Continuity in the Rebuilding of Bombed Cities in Western Europe," *American Journal of Sociology* Vol. LXI, No. 4 (August 1960), pp. 463–469. Amos Hawley presents similar findings for a Japanese city, in "Land Value Patterns in Okayama, Japan, 1940 and 1952," *American Journal of Sociology,* Vol. LX, No. 5 (March 1955).

ment, the federal government should not be subsidizing real estate ventures in the cities when they are "winners." It certainly should not do so if there is no real demand for sites and they are, consequently, "losers."

Aside from CBD development, the "gray areas" of the city are far too vast to be redeveloped profitably. Nor, in general, is there any reason why they should be; they constitute a huge supply of housing, markedly better in quality than the neighborhoods where most of the Negroes and the poor live in contemporary cities. Redistribution of income and taxes between suburbs and central city by means of urban renewal makes no sense if it requires the demolition of such neighborhoods, for there is already a potential demand for them. Eventually, with the "outward" move of Negroes and lower-income populations, a drop in land values should allow the cheap assembly and reuse of the older central neighborhoods—for housing, commerce, parks, or whatever use seems best in the future.

The revitalizing of the "gray areas" should come about through a long-range program to improve the neighborhoods of Negroes and the working-class, who will be the majority of central-city residents for a long time to come. Here the steady upward drift of average income (with the exception of the unemployed) makes new resources systematically available. These resources may be channeled into new working-class residences in the city through several methods. First, as the increase in low-price housing causes the abandonment of the worst substandard housing, it can be demolished and the land reused. Secondly, as new housing opportunities arise for the very poor and the Negroes, a sensible, *minimal* code can be enforced: Older structures without plumbing can be destroyed by the city. Finally, the use of eminent domain can be most profitable in assembling and redeveloping those partially built-up but wholly urbanized areas that were leapfrogged in the earlier growth of the city's housing stock. Such areas, casualties of the speculative bidding of yesteryear, are apt to be "net gainers" for redevelopment; halfway between the CBD and the suburbs, they should find takers.

Again emphasizing the principle that nothing should be destroyed until a superior structure is available for the same use, the local public authorities should use all housing gained by condemnation for temporary relocation. One might even go so far as Sergei Grimm, when he advises the policy of local government's temporarily holding a constant portion of the housing stock—for future highways, redevelopment, parks, schools, and the like.[16] In Grimm's view such housing, held on speculation by government for future *public* use, could be maintained at a minimally acceptable level and profitably used for relocation and public housing, while avoiding the inflated prices of forced purchase. Whether a scheme this radically sensible could be made acceptable to the municipal governments (with their private publics of real estate and business interests) is questionable. The principle, however, is clear: When housing is condemned there should be no rush to turn it into parking lots (a favorite urban renewal strategy) while the people dehoused move to similar housing and push rentals up in the process.

As for the general quality of central-city neighborhoods, esthetically and socially, we must remember the limits imposed by poverty. As a housewife in a Baltimore rehabilitation area said, "There's not too much point in putting too much into this neighborhood. You can't make it as good as you'd like to. Just make it meet the requirements and keep it clean—that's the thing."[17] To bring even this much about, on a city-wide scale, is a project of vast proportions; it requires new housing opportunities, enforcement of a minimal code, and demolition of the worst housing (rolling back the slums), as well as a consistent investment in *public* maintenance and capital improvements. To go beyond this requires skills; communities must be organized and adult education must be a massive program. Millspaugh and Breckenfeld summarize needed instruction.

When the real problems [in the pilot neighborhood] did become apparent, Hearing Board members and Housing Bureau officials listed the main educational needs of the Pilot area residents as follows: (1) simple in-

---

[16] Sergei N. Grimm, "Short Term Housing" (Syracuse, N.Y.: mimeo, n.d.).
[17] Millspaugh and Breckenfeld, *Human Side of Urban Renewal*, p. 21.

struction in the hygiene of housing (2) elementary reading and arithmetic (3) how to prepare a budget (4) how to finance the purchase of a home (5) the privileges and responsibilities of home ownership (6) how to make simple repairs and maintain the home (7) how to secure an honest and competent contractor and how to insure the fulfillment of the contract (8) neighborhood organization and how to deal with City Hall (9) the nature and location of social agencies and the Legal Aid Bureau. As William Brooks, chairman of the Hearing Board put it, "We didn't realize what they needed to know until we got into the hearings.[18]

It seems unlikely that urban renewal will be the vehicle for such a program; neither its chief supporters nor its personnel are committed to "human renewal." Instead, neighborhoods will improve physically with the increase in average income and housing opportunities; socially, the most important drift upward will come about through the superior education and the familiarity with the urban world characteristic of the children who will grow up and leave these neighborhoods.

The legal norms for housing can be raised. The precondition is an increasing supply of low-cost housing; if alternative housing is available at prices that are economically feasible, then minimal housing codes can be uniformly enforced. These codes should be based upon objective criteria and they should be oriented to the requirements for public safety and health—not the esthetic preferences of a given class of Americans. They should probably be enforced by public medical officials, whose expertise and responsibility are widely acceptable. As presently drawn and enforced, the housing codes of most cities produce a moral guerrilla warfare between groups with widely varying norms for housing: to secure agreement and compliance a lowest-common-denominator code, based on manifest public interest, seems the most sensible and equitable standard.

The present codes are biased toward middle-class housing norms and they are rigidly drawn. They must result in discretionary actions by the housing inspectors and courts, and one has the impression that

<hr/>

[18] *Ibid.*, p. 23.

exceptions are more common than the rule. This is a situation conducive to neither public morality nor administrative integrity. At an extreme it results in condemnation of property that is then paid for at rates based on the *illegal uses* that property has had. (This is very much like paying Al Capone the illegal market value for alcohol confiscated by the federal officers.) At the other extreme, rigid enforcement, the poor but struggling homeowner is dehoused by the operation of an *ex post facto* law, a housing standard that means little to him. If housing codes are to be the law of the land, they must be equitable on their face and enforced without discretion. This, again, argues for minimal standards varied systematically for owned versus rented houses and for single-family versus multiple-family dwelling units.

In the long run, urban renewal will make very little difference in the nature and vitality of the central cities. Where the reuse market value of land is high, the program can facilitate the realization of that value. Where it is low, the program will generally avoid commitments, for no LPA official appreciates the jibe that "the federal government is now the biggest grower of ragweed in the country." The federal highway program as it expands freeways, builds arterials and circumferentials, and loops the central city, is a great stimulus to decentralization. In the process older values—financial and otherwise—become obsolete. This may be defined as waste but, as Grimm says:

> In dealing with factors and trends, one must keep in mind certain inherent characteristics of our industrial civilization and of our socioeconomic system. Efficiency and economy are not basic objectives. The Constitution of the United States certainly does not set them up as such, on a par with life, liberty, and the pursuit of happiness. This country is the land of waste, which is the price we pay for liberty and progress.[19]

The declining tax position of the central city is another matter. If the future follows the lines indicated by Vernon and Shussheim, we

---

[19] In *Physical Urban Planning* (Syracuse, New York: School of Architecture, Syracuse University, 1961), p. 76.

can expect the discrepancy between costs and tax-yield to increase continuously. Although it will be mitigated by the steady increase in the income of central-city residents, this will be limited by (1) the pools of unemployed who live in the central city (and whose future is bleak as mechanization increases) and (2) the more general condition; residential property is a tax loser.

The basic need is for a tax income that distributes costs of the central city to those who use it. Brazer has recently suggested that the decline in central-city services stems precisely from the condition in which a fraction of the users, the central-city residents, pay the total cost of everybody's services.[20] This condition can be corrected by some form of use tax, of which the "earnings tax" applying to all who gain income from the central-city's plant and workforce seems the most sensible. A further extension of the Community Facility Loans program, to strengthen the central city's fiscal position, seems a most direct attack on the problem. The desired result, an increase in public moneys for the central city, seems easier to achieve through programs that address it directly than through programs seeking to reverse the entire development of urban complexes.

The Goal of Community Renewal Planning

Urban renewal has increasingly extended in scope. From projects to general neighborhood renewal plans to community renewal programs, the unit of treatment has broadened in response to a growing suspicion that urban areas are interdependencies. Community renewal programs are meant to schedule and program many activities of several sorts over time, so that the joint output will be the renewal

[20] Harvey E. Brazer, "Some Fiscal Implications of Metropolitanism" in *Metropolitan Issues; Social, Governmental, Fiscal,* ed. Guthrie S. Birkhead (Syracuse: The Maxwell Graduate School of Citizenship and Public Affairs, 1962). See also, York Wilburn, "The Changing Ecology of Urban Local Government" in the same volume.

of the entire city. As such, they are subject to all the weaknesses of governmental planning in the United States.

These weaknesses stem from norms prescribing freedom for the private property owner in American society. The "problems" urban renewal faces are the result of land-use commitments originally made as a response to market values. They are complicated by the present governmental fragmentation of the urban area and the resulting tax inequities. The assumption underlying planning is simple: There have been collective losses, suffered as the price of individual freedom to exploit land as the owner desired. Such collective losses may be calibrated in dollars or they may reflect moral or esthetic norms. Insofar as urban renewal can change this situation, introducing rational planning based on foresight and resulting in action, it will affect a revolution in the structure of our urban areas.

But can it? Comprehensive and effective planning for the good, the true, and the beautiful must either work within the narrow limits of the given, or change those limits. The freedom of the property-owner to minimize collective values is clear on every hand: It is apparent in billboards that line the highway through the forest and in the approach to our great cities past dump heaps, shacks, the bone-yards of automobiles, and again, the uncontrolled medley of billboards. One might ask: Why should a people that tolerates these conditions be expected to desire new, well-planned cities? Preference for individual freedom over public welfare shows up on every hand, from the householder who resents a code requiring him to sewer his property to the manufacturer who resents a smoke-abatement ordinance. It is apparent in the resentment of inspectors who are to enforce codes and LPA officials responsible for that enforcement. It is manifest in a legal process that rewards the slum owner and a political system that deifies a Robert Moses, the public entrepreneur who "gets things done."

Should comprehensive renewal programs modify the norm that sees "governmental interference" as an evil, they would still be constricted by others. The intense commitment of Americans to the autonomous power of local government leaves the federal agency working through the local authority. When this is combined with American conservatism respecting the forms of local government, it means that urban renewal works through local government as it is. The LPA is not a new agency with its own powers; it is merely a means of coordinating the existing governmental authorities in a locale. As we have seen, that coordination leaves much to be desired. It is possible only when a public entrepreneur, usually supported by a strong mayor, *creates* the conditions that allow him to work. In the process, elements of a "comprehensive plan" conflicting with his necessary alliances are apt to be expendable, for those who stand for the local planning process are typically without political power.

Planners, who are unable to work effectively within the municipal boundaries of one city, certainly cannot affect the multitude of interacting powers that produce the next temporal stage of the metropolis. The state and federal highway program, basic as it is to area-wide development, is not amenable to local planning control, while outside the city limits in the suburbs there is *no* legal power that forces coordination with the plans of the central city planners. At another level, the counties go merrily on their way, other arms of government with power delegated by the states. Yet if the revitalization of the central cities is to take place, it must be based on the modification or reversal of present decentralizing forces. And, if the rehousing of the poor and the Negroes is to be more than a central-city operation, the effective laws of suburban municipalities must be changed. The housing market is metropolitan in nature and it changes through time. Most master plans pay little attention to those basic conditions.

Even if planners had the powers and those powers had the geographical and functional scope needed for "total planning," it is not certain they have the competence. Discussing the British town planners, Rodwin says:

> The fact is that the town planners' intellectual lines have been overextended: their base needs strengthening; their supplies are limited; they are operating in unknown terrain; and their key personnel are not well enough equipped for many of the problems that lie ahead.
>
> Two of the most glaring weaknesses are in planning education and plan-

ning research. At present the stock of intellectual capital of all town planners is meager. What exists is subject to rapid depreciation. Replenishment
is long overdue. At the same time, British town planners have acquired almost all the tasks and legislative tools they sought. Their increased powers
have brought them to grips with new, complex problems.[21]

Rodwin goes on to point out that this inadequacy is not peculiar to
British planners—it is just that they are suddenly powerful and responsible. Their plans are more than maps: They are to affect action
by the use of the police power and the fisc. Davidoff, Dyckman, and
Mitchell have recently said of American plans, "Most contemporary
city plans are neither sufficiently explicit . . . nor stated in terms of the
nature and rate of change over time in the various parts of the
city."[22]

The problems to which the community renewal programs are addressed, areas of substandard housing and the decline of the CBD,
are the results of markets operating without any over-all planning.
Perhaps they could have been avoided had there been public action
earlier. Now, after they have occurred and become structured through
immense investments in suburbia and central-city slums, with powerful interests active in preserving the governmental walls between sub-
units, the effects are to be undone, not by local initiative, but by a
loose coalition of local forces organized to carry out a federal program. And these local forces are specific to a given municipality—the
central city.

The truth of the matter is, American urban complexes have no integrated governmental structure. The "community" is not reflected
in a unitary polity; it is a loose congeries of governments, each
capable of staying in business with little radical change because nobody expects much of it. Under these circumstances is it reasonable
to expect a federal program to create such a polity? Not, I think,

[21] Lloyd Rodwin, *The British New Towns Policy* (Cambridge: Harvard University Press,
1956), p. 187.
[22] Paul Davidoff, John W. Dyckman and Robert B. Mitchell, "Summary Report on
Objectives of Urban Renewal," presented at Ford Seminar on Urban Renewal, University of Pennsylvania, May 18, 1962.

with leverage gained only through an urban renewal program unknown to most citizens, popular with a few, and increasingly an
object of suspicion to others. But without a unified polity, the community renewal programs can only be a more elaborate form of
central-city slum elimination and redevelopment, with the emphasis
on the latter.

Chapter **8**
THE GREATEST NEED

The urban renewal program lacks the powers necessary to fulfill its radical aims. It also lacks the precedents that could create legitimacy for those aims. It is hemmed in by laws which support the individual's choice of residence and land use, which leave building to the market-place in real estate, which leave action to the local public agency. But its most important limits are, simply, the limits of our knowledge. We have never before faced a wealthy, rapidly changing urban complex, with a determination to mold it into a form suitable to our desires. We do not know enough about the forces producing the metropolis and we know less of the strategems that would allow us to control its growth.

The present program operates with little real knowledge of the housing market. What *are* the effects of demolition of given kinds of housing, in certain areas, within given metropolitan housing markets? What are the effects of rehabilitation, of new building? And, in re-development at the urban core, what are the basic demands for new space and structure? How elastic is the demand, in terms of where that structure is located? What are the alternative supplies? And from this the related questions: What is the total cost, and what the total benefit, of such redevelopment in this center of this metropolis? Most LPAs do not even know the costs and benefits in dollars, much

185

less in the other social values adduced so freely. What are the costs and benefits of centrally sited universities and cultural centers, shopping centers and government centers? How are the costs and benefits distributed—by governmental jurisdiction, by income class and ethnic class?

Of equal importance and greater difficulty, what are the costs and benefits of programs as *among* the more than two hundred metropolitan areas? Their range in wealth and housing is enormous, yet some of the wealthiest are beneficiaries of the present program; some of the poorest are doing little or nothing. In the absence of more knowledge, the program rains on the just and unjust alike, and whatever lies in the soil—rocks, flowers, tares—will probably flourish each in its kind.

Nor do we understand the complex social processes involved in such a radical effort at social control as the Workable Program. What is, indeed, a justifiable and acceptable—therefore enforceable—housing code? On whose standards, with what justification, can it be formulated? And this leads to further unknowns, for the justification of a code must, finally, lie in its effects. What differences does any housing code make in the supply of "decent, safe, and sanitary housing," available to whom? How does this vary by the provisions of the code, and why? What are the steps we must go through when we try to relocate the residents of substandard housing—and what affects their choice, what does not? (A few straws in the wind suggest there is more free play and more complexity in the process then we had guessed.)[1]

It is anomalous. We are willing to spend billions of dollars for radical social action, but almost nothing for knowledge to guide such action and measure its effects. So global is our ignorance that one's

[1]See, for example, Kurt W. Back, *Slums, Projects, and People* (Durham, North Carolina: Duke University Press, 1962) for a thoughtful study of the social and social-psychological mechanisms involved in the move from slums to housing projects in Puerto Rico. The distinction between *housing problems* and human problems in general, for the observer, slum dweller, and relocation official is made clear. The importance of such a distinction is adumbrated in the discussion of slums in Chapter 5.

first reaction might well be to call the whole thing off for a decade or two while we try to understand the nature of the problems.

But this does not seem sensible. The metropolitan areas are flourishing and spreading and the present urban renewal program constitutes a beginning, in authorization and funds and personnel, for an attack on the problems of living in an urban world. Indeed, the present program can provide a powerful lever for the solution of these basic theoretical questions. For the action of social agencies is, formally, similar to that laboratory research which will never be possible on a society—it allows us to control the treatment. Rational intervention into ongoing social systems is the most promising way of gaining efficient knowledge of those systems. But this is true *only* when we know (1) what the preexistent situation was, (2) what the treatment was, and (3) what the effects were. In the case of the present urban renewal program, we are all too often ignorant of all three.

This ignorance is dangerously near sanctification. Governmental action, where programs last over long periods of time, tends toward administrative rigidity. The need for accountability in a federal agency prone to discontinuity in personnel and program tends to produce procedural rigidity, the substitution of documents for known and evaluated action. Thus the Workable Program may become a screen, hiding the true events in the hundreds of cities now experimenting with urban renewal. The cost of such a screen is more than a possible corruption of the program; it is the masking of knowledge. For urban renewal, this globally ambitious excursion into the unknown, must be conceived of as a mass of experiments in the shaping of cities. As experiments, however, the local projects are worthless unless we carefully evaluate their consequences.

What is needed is a greater procedural freedom in the program and a more rigorous evaluation of each project's consequences. The program is a federal program and each LPA is morally and legally responsible for trying to carry out the purposes of the program as conceived in Washington. But in our present state of indecision and ignorance it is a foregone conclusion that some will fail. They fail today and it is not publicly acknowledged—nor do we gain in knowledge from the failure of the experiment. More emphasis upon an evaluation of programs in the light of urban renewal goals should result in greater freedom as well as greater accountability for the local public authorities. They need both.

It is certainly true that the political community varies by city size, that housing needs vary by regions, that housing markets vary widely by both of these factors and by many others. If political problems in small and large cities are very different, the LPAs will have to take them into account; they do so at present. If the supply of low-cost housing varies between cities and *over time,* relocation procedures will vary; they must. If these variations, enormous in magnitude, take place anyway, then the Urban Renewal Agency should vary its requirements systematically, working toward a general theory of public control of change in small cities and large, poor cities and rich.

This is done today through modifying the requirements of the rigid Workable Program. But these adjustments are products of expediency and uncertainty, and in the process all standards may be lost. This is, in part at least, because the standards are unrealistic in the first place, given the jobs they are supposed to do. Conventions should be interpretations of truth and not substitutes for it. Rigid standards and uncontrolled variances produce entirely too many facts by fiat, slums by definition, blight by desire.

Evaluation is possible, however, only if we know what we want to achieve. Here again our lack of knowledge is critical, but it is a different kind of lack; it is not ignorance of facts but uncertainty as to the desired shape of the future city that dogs our intellectual steps. What, indeed, do we want of the metropolis? And what price are we willing to pay? Dyckman and Isaacs have recently concluded that to renew all American cities within a twelve-year period (by the current theory of urban renewal) would cost approximately *one trillion dollars.*[2] Is anyone seriously interested in such a program?

On the other hand, I recall a trip through Jerome, Arizona, an old copper mining town in the mountains near Prescott. It was a ghostly

[2] John W. Dyckman and Reginald R. Isaacs, with the assistance of Peter R. Senn, *Capital Requirements for Urban Development and Renewal* (New York: McGraw-Hill Book Co., Inc., 1961).

experience; this city of 15,000 people had been abandoned as recently as 1953, and the houses with their flowerbeds, the stores with their signs, the streets, sidewalks, utilities, all lay against the mountainside as useless as boulders and gravel slides. The social waste was almost tangible. Should all Americans have their present heart's desires, would the central city of our metropolis begin to resemble Jerome? And would we be prepared to assume that cost?

If this analysis is correct, we shall neither abandon the central city nor recreate the centrality of an older day. Instead, the center will gradually evolve into the municipality of the working class and the ethnic. Here they will have their most forcible representation in politics; the demands growing out of their ways of life will be registered in the central-city polity. However, as the slums are rolled back the area of central land available at a low price should allow the beginning of massive privately financed housing developments, valuable not because of the "glamor" of downtown, but because the center is the point of easiest access to the entire metropolitan area. As decentralization continues, a site near the great interchange will have a real value to those who wish to use the metropolis as one unit, whether for financial, social, or other reasons.

It is likely that a new esthetic of cities is developing, even at present. The enormous spread of Los Angeles is divided into superblocks by freeways; the giant grid overlies arterials which meet in the center. The entire metropolis is moving toward a situation in which giant subcenters organize most of life for most citizens, while movement is easy from one end of the area to the other. Though many observers shudder at Los Angeles as the city of the future, the city grows and its inhabitants make do. They have the fewest slums of any of our great cities. Even the Negro citizens are the most fortunate in the country with respect to housing and many other amenities. Should they be able to organize and participate in the urban polity (and the Watts' incidents demonstrate how insensitive that polity is at present), they would be the most fortunate in the country in many respects. Still the average Angelenos have easy access to metropolis, mountains, deserts, beaches; they have reasons, as familistic Americans, to be grateful to the giant gridirons of energy, transportation, and communication that allow them such freedom of choice. And in their acculturation to a new kind of city, their images change:

> On fast roads, one can have some sense of the major topography. One subject felt that coming over a great hill each morning marked the midpoint of her journey and gave shape to it. Another noted the extension of the city's scale due to the new roads, which have changed her whole conception of the relations of elements. There were references to the pleasure of momentary extensive views from elevated portions of the freeway, versus the contained monotonous sensation of the embankment or a cut.[3]

So much for the larger picture, the image of the public space created by our common actions. It is a space without a single dominant center, but a space with many subcenters specialized by use and by kinds of people. And, in the greater part of the urbanized space, in the interstices between freeways, the neighborhoods spread their lots and houses, a spectrum of opportunities for the average man with his commitment to family, home, neighborhood, and friends—

> . . . people took great delight in flowers and vegetation, which indeed are the glory of many of the residential sections of the city. The early portions of home-to-work trips were full of vivid pictures of the flowers and trees. Even car drivers moving at high speed seemed to note and enjoy such urban detail.[4]

It is by no means certain that Los Angeles does not approximate the "golden mean" of the cities desired by most Americans. If this is so, the attempt to recreate the central city as it once was had better be abandoned, for it cannot possibly succeed.

The Heavenly City and the Earthly City

There have been dramatic instances of urban redevelopment in the past. Cities have been rebuilt to patterns of grandeur and charm. Baron Haussman's Paris, Pericles' Athens, some of the Italian city

[3]Kevin Lynch, *The Image of the City*, pp. 42–43.
[4]*Ibid.*, p. 43.

states come immediately to mind. But these achievements were only possible because of the power and wealth of a single (and ruthless) governor. There is no "Prince" in the American way of life; our political culture continually reinforces our glorification of the private sphere. We invest our treasures in our private lives and in that private space called "the home," with a consequent disregard for public space, public achievement, and public action.

The age-old base for a comely and orderly city is in the *vernacular,* the folk-language of taste in a society. Where the proper nature of buildings is known to all, agreed upon by all, and where that archetype is fortunate in its proportions and textures, the society may automatically produce pleasing collective artifacts. Its villages and cities may inspire admiration in the sophisticated architect or planner from a much more "advanced" society. We have remnants of such vernacular achievements in America today; the Vieux Carré in New Orleans, the Federalist structures in Philadelphia and Georgetown, the scattered traces of the Spanish era in Monterey, all bear dramatic evidence of the powerful controls and the resulting order of simpler societies. (Even Williamsburg, though resembling "a stuffed crow under glass," according to the poet, Barker, is still a paragon of stylistic achievement in contemporary America.) Ironic evidence that these survivals are valued, they attract a multimillion-dollar tourist trade. Yet they were not expensive to build, could in fact be rebuilt now. (One official in the code enforcement agency of New Orleans suggested as much; he felt that half the Vieux Carré should be bulldozed out as substandard housing.) All they have is style and craft.

And perhaps our main achievements in urban order will be, for a long time, simply the result of our vernacular. In city after city the most memorable experience of the visitor is not the massed office buildings and hotels of the central business district, but the miles of pleasant neighborhoods planted like huge collective gardens, providing the setting for that small-scale family living so dear to Americans. When such neighborhoods emerge through the efforts of large-scale developers, one has a kind of combination of "the Prince" and the vernacular. Street system, land use, drainage, relations with the larger network of transportation, all can be planned by the merchant prince in ways impossible for a gaggle of single-house contractors. Effective public planning of great cities as units is nonexistent in this country today and probably quite impossible, but in the "middle range" impressive achievements have occurred through the private market. The scale of development, however acquired, seems to be the key to the thing. Such shopping complexes as Lloyd's Center in Portland or Old Orchard in Chicago would be universally praised except for one thing—they are not in the central business district.

Meanwhile the only effective planners in our cities are those who lay out the giant grid of the freeways. Their creations, beautiful in themselves, loop together the urban worlds of the spreading metropolis, allowing those who scatter to revisit the centers of their childhood. And at the center, in the truly massive cities, the aggregation of towers, bridges, ramps, and malls is indeed powerful. It is a creation unplanned, comparable in its form and its creation to the Grand Canyon rather than Florence. The processes of the market are as blind to the grandeur of the final product as the forces of erosion in the Arizona desert; each reflects an order of a kind.

Index of Proper Names

General Index

Aid for Dependent Children, 57
American Association of Social
    Workers, 128
American Association of University
    Women, 128
American Federation of Labor
    (A F of L), 128
American Municipal Association, 158
American Public Health Association,
    21, 22, 46, 102, 128
    Housing Code, 102
American Society of Planning
    Officials, xiii
American Veterans of World War II
    (AMVETS), 128
Athens, Greece, 190

Back of the Yards, 55, 168
Baltimore, Maryland, 23, 74, 177
Baton Rouge, Louisiana, 66
Big Nine, 102
Blight, 7, 10, 18, 19, 20, 21, 22, 23,
    24, 28, 29, 30, 31, 32, 33, 35, 36,
    45, 52, 78, 81, 93, 96, 112, 115,
    118, 119, 126, 138, 154, 155, 160,
    161, 169

Boston, Massachusetts, x, 132, 144
    Collins, (Mayor), 37
    Development Program, 53
    Industrial Committee of Chamber
        of Commerce, 93
    West End Project, xi, 40, 59, 60, 77,
        92, 120, 121, 145, 146, 149
Bronx (New York City), 126
Brookings Institution, 56
Brooklyn (New York City), 126
Bureau of Budget, 107
Bureau of Building Inspection, 98

Capital, 35, 74, 75, 120, 177
    Improvements, 74, 75, 177
    Investment, 35
Cardinal's Committee on Conserva-
    tion, 128
Central Business District (CBD), 8,
    27, 28, 31, 32, 33, 69, 80, 82, 85,
    91, 92, 94, 96, 97, 113, 114, 118,
    122, 123, 126, 129, 130, 135, 136,
    137, 138, 139, 154, 156, 157, 158,
    159, 160, 161, 165, 174, 176, 183
Chicago, Illinois, x, 47, 55, 74, 118,
    121, 132, 174